So, You Wish to Learn All About Economics?

A Text on Elementary Mathematical Economics

So, You Wish to Learn All About Economics?

A Text on Elementary Mathematical Economics

by Lyndon H. LaRouche, Jr.

New Benjamin Franklin House
New York, 1984

Also by the author:
There Are No Limits to Growth
Imperialism: The Final Stage of Bolshevism
The Final Defeat of Ayatollah Khomeini
Why Revival of SALT Won't Stop War
Basic Economics for Conservative Democrats
What Every Conservative Should Know About Communism
Will The Soviets Rule During the 1980's?
How to Defeat Liberalism and William F. Buckley
The Power of Reason: A Kind of Autobiography
The Ugly Truth About Milton Friedman
  with David P. Goldman

About the Author:
LaRouche: Will This Man Become President?
  by the editors of the Executive Intelligence Review

This book is designed as the companion text to a two-and-a-half-hour
LaRouche television special, "The Power of Labor."

So, You Wish to Learn All About Economics?
© 1984 by New Benjamin Franklin House

FIRST EDITION

For information, address the publisher:
The New Benjamin Franklin House Publishing Company, Inc.
304 West 58th Street, 5th floor
New York, New York 10019
(212) 247-7484

ISBN: 0-933488-35-1

Cover: Virginia Baier
Cover photograph: The U.S. Space Shuttle, courtesy of the U.S. National
Aeronautics and Space Administration.

Printed in the United States of America

Contents

Foreword

This book has two distinct, but interrelated functions. In its own right, it is a university textbook on the shaping of national economic policy from the standpoint of modern mathematical economics, exposing the principal reasons Econometrics, Operations Research, and Systems Analysis have accumulated so consistent a record of failures. Since the text deals with the making of policies of national governments, such as the United States', it also serves as a manual for use by government officials and leading advisors to government on these matters.

Since the author is presently a candidate for the Democratic Party's 1984 U.S. presidential nomination, were he to be elected President, or his influence upon the President to be considerable in this policy area, the text gives excellent forewarning of what the policies of the United States might become. It is this latter implication, and its obvious implications, in turn, which prompted the initial circulation of a xeroxed, limited edition to appropriate selections of recipients.

February 1984

Preface

By Lyndon H. LaRouche, Jr.

The author is chief executive for an international,
specialist newsweekly, the *Executive Intelligence
Review*, whose quarterly forecast for the U.S.
economy has been the most accurate in the history of economics.

The first known writing on the subject of economics is the
Judeo-Christian Book of Genesis. In Genesis, man is informed
that he shall not live but by means of his daily labor. He is
also instructed to be fruitful, to multiply the human population, to fill up the earth, and to exert command over all
creatures and objects of nature. Excellent advice: No society
which rejects those instructions would last for long.

Economic science is a more recent development. The
first economic scientist, in the strict modern sense of science,
was Gottfried Leibniz, who also was the first to produce a
differential calculus,[1] and also more branches of modern science than most of today's university graduates could list from
memory of their names.[2] The idea of developing an economic
science did not begin with Leibniz; the case of Leonardo da
Vinci's work on the theory of design of machinery, and other
examples show that the effort to develop an economic science
was well under way by the close of the fifteenth century. By
the beginning of the seventeenth century, work in this direction was most commonly called *cameralism*. In fact, until the
early nineteenth century some German universities were still
teaching Leibniz's principles of economic science as part of

a program of training in cameralism; in that curriculum, Leibniz's economics is listed under the title of Physical Economy.
Leibniz's development of economic science began with
a paper published in 1671, *Society and Economy,* on the
subject of the necessary costs and wages of productive labor.
His work continued with intensive study of the principles of
heat-powered machinery; out of Leibniz's work on this subject
he developed the terms *work* and *power,* as those terms came
to be used in physical science after him. In the same connection, Leibniz defined the meaning of the term *technology,* a
term translated into French as *polytechnique.*

During the eighteenth century, the influence of Leibniz's economic science was strong in many parts of Europe,
and spilled into circles around Benjamin Franklin in America.
Leibniz developed a comprehensive program for developing
the mines and industries of Russia, in his capacity as advisor
to Czar Peter I; until the policy was reversed, during the last
part of the eighteenth century, the industrial output of Russia
exceeded that of Britain. Most of the leading scientists of
Germany, into the early nineteenth century, were developed
at technical schools and universities based on Leibniz's program. In France, Leibniz's science was adopted by circles
associated with the Oratorian teaching order, and was the
basis for the establishment of the École Polytechnique in France,
in 1794, under the leadership of Franklin's former collaborator, Lazare Carnot. And so on.

Over the period from 1791 through about 1830, Leibniz's economic science became identified world-wide as the
American System of political economy. This name was coined
by U.S. Treasury Secretary Alexander Hamilton, in 1791,
within a U.S. policy document submitted to Congress entitled
"A Report on the Subject of Manufactures." After the end
of the War of 1812, the circles around Lazare Carnot and
the Marquis de Lafayette collaborated intimately with leading
circles in the United States, especially through channels of the
U.S. military freemasonic association which the Marquis de

Lafayette led in Europe, the Society of the Cincinnati. A close former associate of both Franklin's and Hamilton's, Philadelphia publisher Mathew Carey, led the revival of Hamilton's economic policies in pulling the United States out of a deep economic depression at that time. Lafayette introduced a German economist, Friedrich List, to Carey; List later organized the German Customs Union (*Zollverein*) which made the nineteenth-century industrial development of Germany possible. The leading U.S. economist of the mid-nineteenth century was Mathew Carey's son, Henry C. Carey. Henry Clay and his Whig Party were committed to the Hamilton-Carey-List American System as U.S. economic policy, as was the Clay-Carey Whig, President Abraham Lincoln. Beginning approximately 1868, the American System was introduced as policy to Japan, partly through an economist closely associated with Henry C. Carey, E. Peshine Smith; Smith served as economic consultant to the Meiji Restoration in Japan during most of the 1870s, laying the basis on which Japan emerged as a modern industrial power.

About the same time Leibniz was developing economic science, the Jesuit order and its trainees began first steps toward developing a counter-teaching. Jesuit-trained William Petty, head of the London Royal Society and head of Britain's banking affairs during the late seventeenth century, was the starting-point for this in Britain. Earlier English economic thinking had been cameralist since Henry VII, in the same direction as the economic policies of Jean-Baptiste Colbert during the late seventeenth century in France. In France, the Jesuits directly produced what became known as the Physiocratic doctrine, explicitly modeling their work on the economy of China; Dr. Quesnay is the prototype of this development. The Jesuit schools of political economy in Britain, France, and elsewhere focused their attack against *colbertisme*.

Formal British political economy began with Adam Smith's *Wealth of Nations*. Smith's work in this direction began as a follower of David Hume; during the late 1750s, Smith taught Hume's philosophy at the University of Glasgow, where he wrote his 1759 *Theory of the Moral Sentiments*. In 1763, Smith was picked up by a direct descendant of William Petty, the Second Earl of Shelburne. In a famous carriage ride during that year,[3] Shelburne gave Smith instructions on a program for wrecking simultaneously the economy of France and those of the English colonies in North America; the highlights of that program were later featured in the *Wealth of Nations*. Smith picked up his economics traveling in France and Switzerland, chiefly from Dr. Quesnay and allied circles.

After Smith, the most prominent British political economist was Jeremy Bentham, also a leading protégé of Lord Shelburne. Bentham's 1789 *Introduction To The Principles of Morals and Legislation,* and his 1787 "In Defence of Usury," are Bentham's most relevant writings on political economy. During Bentham's period, all influential study and teaching of political economy in Britain was concentrated at the British East India Company's training center at Haileybury, with which Bentham himself was closely associated. This was the center which produced Thomas Malthus, David Ricardo, James Mill, and John Stuart Mill. Lord Shelburne was the leading political representative of the British East India Company's interests at that time, who struck an agreement with George III, under which the Company took over the government of England, with help of the Company's own bank, Baring Brothers; the long government of Shelburne's puppet, Prime Minister William Pitt the Younger, was the result.[4]

So, following the 1815 Congress of Vienna, or during the years immediately following, there were only two significant, and directly opposing doctrines of political economy in the world: the American System versus the British East India Company's teachings. In the United States, through the 1860s, the American System was the policy of the Whigs, Whig Democrats, and Republicans, whereas the British system was the policy of the New England Abolitionists, the New

York financial Establishment, the leaders of the Confederacy's movement, and of Jackson, Van Buren, Polk, Pierce, Buchanan, and the Democratic Party king-maker of the 1850s and 1860s, New York's August Belmont. With the adoption of the U.S. Specie Resumption Act of the middle to late 1870s, this Act bankrupted the United States' government, caused a deep and prolonged economic depression, with massive social upheavals, and created the successive waves of financial panics, through the 1907 Panic, leading into the formation of the Federal Reserve System. With the establishment of the Federal Reserve System, put through by the election of President Woodrow Wilson, the United States was placed under the regimen of the British System. Meanwhile, through the ruining of the U.S. currency by the U.S. Specie Resumption Act, the balance of financial and economic power was tilted in the world to the point that the British gold standard took control of world trade, and London, in partnership with the Dutch, Swiss, and Venice-Genoa banking interests, established a virtual world dictatorship of the British system of political economy.

For these historical reasons, what is generally taught in universities throughout most of the world today is either the British system of political economy or some outgrowth of that system. This includes Marxian political economy. Although Karl Marx was a product of Giuseppe Mazzini's Young Europe, and anti-capitalist by political profession, his dogma was derived entirely from the Physiocrats and the British East India Company teachings, which Marx defended rather fanatically against Friedrich List and Henry C. Carey.[5] Marxian political economy is properly treated as a legitimate branch of British political economy, whenever the British is contrasted with the American System. Today, although many universities teach Marx's economics as part of the economics curriculum, virtually no study of the work of the early cameralists, of Leibniz, of Chaptal, Ferrier, Dupin, or of Hamilton, the Careys, and List is included in the curriculum; these adversaries of the British system are more or less totally blacked out, to the extent that many professional economists do not even know the names of many of the leading economists of the sixteenth, seventeenth, eighteenth, and nineteenth centuries, and nothing of the economic science of Leibniz.

Since the refutation of the British doctrines of political economy is accomplished in various published locations, including those of the Careys, List, and E. Peshine Smith, as well as the author's own,[6] we shall not repeat that here. Our purpose here is to introduce the ABCs of economic science positively, a task which permits us to disregard safely the British System and its outgrowths. The foregoing remarks serve to situate the matter to which we now turn our attention.

NOTES

1. Gottfried Leibniz's differential calculus was sent to a Paris printer in 1676, nearly a dozen years before the appearance of Newton's version. Moreover, Newton's fluxions doctrine is not actually a differential calculus, as Leibniz points out in his own *Origins of the Calculus* and the Leibniz-Clarke correspondence. The specifications for a differential calculus's development were stipulated by Johannes Kepler. The principal work leading into Leibniz's solution to this specified task was accomplished by Blaise Pascal's development of differential number theory, deriving differential number series from principles of geometry. It was Pascal's work on differential numbers, intersecting Leibniz's own earlier explorations of such series, which led directly to the formulation of the differential calculus. These requirements are not satisfied by Newton's doctrine, to the effect that Newton's techniques were dropped in favor of Leibniz's.

2. There are still approximately 100,000 chiefly unexplored pages of Leibniz's manuscript in the archive, each portion of which turns up more or less important work by Leibniz on some branch of scientific inquiry.

3. The carriage ride is documented in the Smith family biography.

4. Shelburne was prevented from assuming the position himself, because his training by the Jesuits was too well known among English Protestant circles.

5. Although Marx did plagiarize significantly from both List and Henry C. Carey, in matters which he or Friedrich Engels each claimed to involve Marx's own original discoveries. "Labor-power" is a notion originally circulated by Leibniz, and is defined as "increase of the productive powers of labor" in Hamilton's 1791 "On the Subject of Manufactures," in which Hamilton refutes the physiocratic and other doctrines of A. Turgot's *Reflections,* from which much of Smith's *Wealth of Nations* was plagiarized. This is central to the published work of List which Marx attacked. The analysis of the social division of labor was elaborated by Henry C. Carey in the 1837 edition of his *Principles of Political-Economy,* and appears in works which Marx read and attacked later. However, Marx adapted the plagiarized conceptions to his version of the British system of Smith and Ricardo, and also to Dr. Quesnay's doctrine.

6. Mathew Carey, in *Addresses of the Philadelphia Society,* 1819; Friedrich List, *The National System of Political-Economy* (1844); Henry C. Carey, *Principles of Political-Economy* (1840); E. Peshine Smith, *A Manual of Political Economy* (1853). See also Lyndon H. LaRouche, Jr. and David P. Goldman, *The Ugly Truth About Milton Friedman,* New York, 1980.

CHAPTER 1

Leibniz's Approach to Economic Science

The significant feature of the heat-powered machine is the functional relationship between increase of the power supplied to such machines and the increase of the operatives' *power* to accomplish *work*. From the examination of this functional relationship, Gottfried Leibniz (1646–1716) defined the notions of *power, work,* and *technology* within physical science.

The study of this functional relationship, extended from the specific case of the heat-powered machine, to all other features of the productive process, constitutes the subject-matter of *Physical Economy*. Physical Economy is an integral feature of physical science as a whole; the study of political economy in a manner everywhere governed by principles of physical economy, is *economic science*.

The practical setting for Leibniz's development of economic science was his intention that mining, manufacturing, and water transportation should be revolutionized by general use of coal-powered steam engines. Leibniz's collaborator, Denis Papin (1647–1714), was the first to develop a successful steam engine, an engine which successfully powered a river boat.[1] Leibniz explained that the development of manufacturing based on coal-fired steam engines required a qualitative improvement in the mining of coal and ores. This improvement required the application of the steam engine to such mining applications as pumping water, as a precondition for the application of coal-fired potentialities to manufacturing. This was the kernel of the economic program which Leibniz

1

Gottfried Leibniz

supplied to Russia's Peter I—which is why Russia grew to surpass Britain in scale of development of mining and manufacturing during the course of the eighteenth century. The revolution in mining prompted by Leibniz's influence radiated from cameralist centers in Germany to North and South America, and into the development of Japan.[2]

Although Leibniz's first writing on political economy, *Society and Economy,* was written in 1671, his work on principles of heat-powered machinery began during the period in Paris, 1672–1676, in which he worked in a scientific institution created by French statesman Jean-Baptiste Colbert (1619–1683), Mazarin's associate and successor. Among the most significant of Leibniz's associates during that period was another protégé of Colbert's, Christiaan Huyghens (1629–1695), whose approach to development of powered machinery we recognize today in the principles of the gasoline and diesel internal combustion engine.

The development of modern steam-powered machin-

In 1690, the first steam engine with cylinder and piston was developed by Denis Papin, Leibniz's collaborator, who in 1707 (above) ran the first steamboat.

ery dates from the late fifteenth-century work of Leonardo da Vinci (1452–1519). The effort to develop coal as an industrial fuel was in progress during the late sixteenth century, in English circles associated with the great scientist William Gilbert (1544–1603).[3] Of more fundamental significance for Leibniz's development of economic science, Leonardo elaborated the principles of design of machinery, elaborating the basis for the work of Huyghens, Leibniz and, later, the École Polytechnique of Lazare Carnot (1753–1823) and Gaspard Monge (1746–1818). Leibniz's *Principle of Least Action,* which we shall discover here to have been the center of his definition of *technology* (French: *polytechnique*), is derived from the geometrical principles of machine design employed by da Vinci.

The Principle of Least Action is so central to economic science that a few words about the development of the related geometrical principles must be situated at this point in the text.

Relative to every known period of history, the pace of development of physical science in Europe from the fifteenth century through the middle of the nineteenth is orders of magnitude greater than in any other period, or any other branch of human culture. To the extent this can be credited significantly to the contributions by any individual scientist, the entirety of the achievements of modern mathematical physics, in particular, would not have been possible without the work accomplished by Cardinal Nicolaus of Cusa (1401–1463) in such influential writings as *De Docta Ignorantia* (*On Learned Ignorance*). Cusa stipulated a solar hypothesis which, in modified version, was employed and proven by Johannes Kepler (1571–1630), the founder of modern mathematical physics.[4] Of most direct bearing on the origins of Leibniz's Principle of Least Action, Cusa revolutionized geometry in the course of a thorough re-working of Archimedes' (circa 287 to 212 B.C.) quadrature of the circle; Cusa announced he had discovered a method superior to Archimedes', a discovery known today as *the isoperimetric theorem of topology,* called by Cusa a *minimum-maximum principle.* This discovery was the basis for Leibniz's Principle of Least Action, the key to measurement of technology. The same discovery, in the more advanced form it was employed by Karl Gauss (1777–1855), Lejeune Dirichlet (1805–1859), and Bernhard Riemann (1826–1866), is the basis for the LaRouche-Riemann method of economic analysis, the subject of this text.

Prior to the production of what is known today as Euclid's Thirteen Books, *The Elements,* in Egypt, classical Greek geometry had been of the form called today *synthetic geometry.* It is a form of geometry which excludes all axioms, postulates, and the formal-deductive methods of proof associated with Euclid's theorems. The only self-evident form of existence in synthetic geometry is circular action; the definitions of straight line and point are derived from the folding of a circle against itself. With only circular action, plus the line and point so defined, every other figure in geometry must be produced by construction, using nothing but these three elements. Cusa's rediscovery that circular action is a self-evident form of existence in visible space, the isoperimetric proof, revolutionized European geometry among such followers of Cusa as Luca Pacioli (1450–1520), and Pacioli's collaborator Leonardo da Vinci. The work of Cusa, Pacioli, Leonardo, and such followers of Leonardo as Albrecht Dürer (1471–1528) and the School of Raphael (Raffaello Sanzio, 1483–1520), was the basis for the work of Kepler, Gérard Desargues (1591–1661), Pierre Fermat (1601–1665), and Blaise Pascal (1623–1662), all directly or indirectly essential contributors to the work of Leibniz. The work of Gauss, Dirichlet, and Riemann is based upon this same geometrical method.[5]

The central feature of the work on geometry by Pacioli and Leonardo, was the mastery of the principle of the Five Platonic Solids, from Plato's (circa 427 to 347 B.C.) *Timaeus* dialogue.[6] This is the proof that in visible ("Euclidean") space, only five species of regular polyhedra can be constructed by methods of synthetic geometry. These five are: 1) the regular tetrahedron, 2) cube, 3) octahedron, 4) twelve-sided duodecahedron, and 5) twenty-sided icosahedron. 1), 3), and 5) have faces which are each equal equilateral triangles; the duodecahedron's faces are each equal regular pentagons. Pacioli constructed a proof of this theorem in his *The Divine Proportions (Divine Proportione,* 1494). A more rigorous proof was developed by Leonhard Euler (1707–1783), a proof which is at the center of Euler's development of topology on the basis of Leibniz's *analysis situs.* It is readily proven that each of the other four Platonic solids is derived from the duodecahedron; it is also shown, in this connection, that the Golden Section, the synthetic-geometrical construction employed to construct a regular pentagon or duodecahedron, is the characteristic feature of the uniqueness of the Five Platonic Solids.

The design of the Athens Acropolis is a striking demonstration of the fact that Plato's contemporaries and predecessors of classical Greece used a synthetic geometry centered upon the Golden Section. Also, comparing the work of Albrecht Dürer with the harmonic ratios employed in design of the Acropolis, it is shown that these classical Greeks understood the principle rediscovered by Pacioli and Leonardo da Vinci, that *all living processes are essentially distinguished geometrically from non-living by the fact that the morphology of growth, and of growth-determined functions, of living processes is that of a self-similar pattern of growth, such that the self-similarity is in a harmonic ratio congruent with the Golden Section.*

Admittedly, various cults have attempted to read mystical properties into the pentagon and Golden Section for such reasons. There is nothing mystical involved, if one knows the relevant work of Gauss and Riemann, for example. Before this text is completed, the reader will understand the rudiments of the matter, and their indispensable function in economic science, free of all mystification. For the purposes of the present section of the text, it is sufficient to touch upon only a few leading points bearing directly on Leibniz's discoveries in economic science.

First, the significance of the Golden Section's relationship to morphology of living processes begins to make sense once it is recognized why what is called a *Fibonacci series* (Leonardo of Pisa, who was probably about thirty or so years of age when he wrote his 1202 *Liber Abaci*) converges upon the values determined by the Golden Section. A Fibonacci series is a geometrical series (geometrically determined series

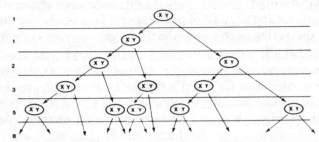

Growth in accordance with the Fibonacci series, in which each number is the sum of the two preceding numbers (1, 2, 3, 5, 8...). In the simple case above, the assumption is made that every pair (xy) lives for two generations and produces one pair of young during each generation. Each of these pairs lives for two generations and dies after producing the second pair of young. If, additionally, each pair of young consists of a male and female animal, which again produce two generations of young, then the growth of this animal population corresponds to the Fibonacci series.

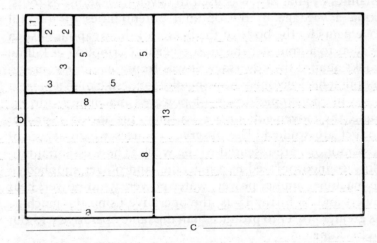

In the Fibonacci rectangle, the proportions (short side to long side) of the ordered rectangles approach the proportion of the golden section, a:b = b:c, where a is the short side of a given rectangle, and b the long side, which is also the length of the short side of a new rectangle whose long side is c.

of whole numbers) which accurately estimates population growth, including growth of populations of cells. As the numbers in the series become modestly large, the ratios defined converge rapidly upon the values of the Golden Section. It requires only rather simple observation of plants to prove afresh Pacioli's and da Vinci's discovery for plant life. Leonardo's work on anatomy of people, horses, and so forth was chiefly a scientific study of the same principle of the Golden Section.[7] Not only are the forms of the human body, for example, determined by the principle of the Golden Section; the dynamics of the morphology of bodily function are also determined so.

Among the numerous branches of modern science founded by Leonard da Vinci, chiefly on the basis of these geometrical principles, Leonardo applied his studies of anatomical dynamics for design of weapons, tools, and machinery. In design of weapons, for example, knowledge of the dynamics of anatomy was used to develop weapons as tools, taking advantage of the optimal potentialities of forceful movements by the body of the bearer of the weapon, in such a way as to administer the most efficiently crippling or killing attacks against the adversary. It was from this same vantage-point that he developed the principles for design of machinery.

In the simple design of powered machinery, for example, the movements of the workman producing a kind of product are studied. The observer adduces which aspect of those motions are essential to the work. These essential motions are incorporated in a machine, and power supplied to the machine: animal power, water power, wind power, heat power, and so forth. Thus, the operative using the machine has greater power to produce than the same operative without the machine.

However, generally speaking, the power applied to the work by a machine is not the same power supplied to the machine as a whole. A very simple machine, a simple knife blade, illustrates the point: the pressure applied by the sharpened edge of the blade is vastly greater than the pressure exerted upon the handle of the knife. *The power is more concentrated.* We measure such concentration of power as increase of *energy-flux density.* This measures the concentration of power per centimeter of movement, or per square meter of cross-section of action, or per cubic meter of volume of action. If one ton of impulse is supplied to a machine, and this impulse is concentrated a thousand times on a work area, a maximum of one thousands of tons of impulse is applied to the work area. In our text, we shall most frequently measure energy-flux density in kilowatts, and measure kilowatts per square kilometer or per square meter.

The first measurement of the effects of machine design is comparison of the human effort required to operate the machine and the amount of work accomplished by the operator employing the machine. If the machine is powered by means other than human muscular effort, we must measure the cost of producing the animal power, water power, wind power, or heat power in terms of the human effort by society to organize, and to deliver such power to the machine. This latter we may view as the capital cost of supplying the power. *We must then compare changes in the ratio of capital cost per operative associated with use of a particular class of machinery, with changes in the rate of work-output by the operative employing the machine.*

This comparison leads to a mathematical function. Imagine a graph, in which the Y axis measures rate of work output per operative, and the X axis measures increasing value of the capital cost of power supplied per operative. Next, expand the mathematical function, by adding a Z axis. This measures increase of the energy-flux density of effort applied by the machine. Until a later part of this text, our references to a mathematical function of this type will signify the three-dimensional function identified here.

In the transmission of input-power to the work, through the machine, some of the power is lost as "waste heat" or the equivalent. The ratio of loss is a subject of special interest to us as we increase significantly the concentration of power, the energy-flux density of the effort applied to work. There is an amusing, curious consideration which confronts us here. We tend to accomplish much higher rates of work with the higher energy-flux density of a fraction of the total power supplied to the machine, than with the entire power supplied at relatively much lower energy-flux density. It appears that less power accomplishes more work than a greater amount of power: that is one of the curious features of economic science which bear more or less directly upon the fundamental features of economic science.

The additional general feature of the mathematical function which interests us greatly, is the phenomenon of "diminishing rates of return." At what points do increases of the capital-cost ratio per operative, or of the energy-flux density, cease to afford us the same rate of increase of output as during preceding levels of growth of capital-cost intensity, or energy-flux density, or both combined?

The same principles apply to the case of agriculture.

We measure the output of agriculture in two ways: 1) output per operative, and 2) output per hectare or square kilometer. In first approximation, we measure the output itself in such terms as bushels of grain, tons of edible animal-product, and so forth. Ultimately, in economics, we must measure these products as components of a "market-basket." There are two "market-baskets": 1) capital goods per employed operative of agriculture, manufacturing, construction, mining, and transportation; 2) consumer goods per capita required by households. By using "market-baskets" as a standard of measurement of product, the output of production is compared with the required inputs of the society effecting that production. Production must be correlated with the total number of square kilometers occupied by that society; this is a measurement of the per-square-kilometer rate of productive activity by the society, a measurement affiliated with the notion of energy-flux density. The two measures, per square kilometer and per capita (per operative) are combined by the link of population density.

The case of agriculture illustrates the way in which principles adduced from study of the principles of heat-powered machines apply to economic processes in the most general way.

The significance of the heat-powered machine within the economic process as a whole is measured by the yardstick of *economy of total (and average) human effort.* The image of this measurement is conveyed by the notion of providing the same market-basket per capita with less effort by society as a whole, and that the content of the market-basket may be improved in quantity and quality without increasing the outlay of effort by society. In other words, labor-saving methods are the kernel of the result to be measured in political economy. This is the yardstick properly employed for *National Income Accounting.*[8]

We have already reported that the general use of the combustion of coal—to replace reliance on burning of wood, on water power, on wind power—to power machinery, was the benchmark adopted by Leibniz for his founding of economic science. We have already identified leading features of the mathematical function required. The cost of production of coal is to be compared with the benefit obtained by burning that coal to power machinery. The function of the heat-powered machine, according to Leibniz, is to enable an operative using a heat-powered machine to accomplish the work-output of "a hundred others" lacking use of such a machine. *The labor-saving represented* (economy of labor) must be compared with the cost of the machine and its coal consumption. The cost of coal consumption includes mining and transporting that coal, and also the costs of combustion required to convert coal into a power source for the machine.

In our initial description of the mathematical function required, a few paragraphs earlier, we defined the function in the terms of reference appropriate for comparison of machines with one another. We must restate that mathematical function now. Let A be the labor-saving obtained by improvements in productive powers of labor through heat-powered machinery, and let B represent the additional costs to society of producing, maintaining, and powering the machinery; it is the per capita value of $(A - B = C)$, where C signifies the margin of net gain to society, which must be considered in defining the terms of the Y axis. This gain, C, becomes a new level of per capita output (and consumption) by society, becoming an enlargement of the per capita marketbasket. At what levels of increase of capital intensity and increase of energy-flux density does this function show "diminishing" return?

Capital intensity is approximated as the ratio of the amount of labor consumed (per machine operative) as capital, to the labor of the average machine operative. The capital costs included for determining this ratio include the labor required to produce and maintain the machine, to supply its power, but not such items of "overhead expense" as administration, non-scientific forms of services, selling costs, financial charges, and so forth.

As capital intensity increases, what is the correlated rate of increase of average productivity of labor in the society as a whole? Or, compare only the increase of productive powers of labor of only the employed operatives' component of the total labor force. In fact, both measures of increase of average per capita productivity should correlate.

The "curve" of our mathematical function, as described by correlating increases in capital intensity with average productivity of labor, is a "curve" describing *increase of the power to accomplish work*. We must perform the same expansion of the function we specified for the machine, a few paragraphs earlier; we must add the Z axis, increase of energy-flux density. We have, then, a "curve" which describes "diminishing returns" at some point for capital intensity, for the condition that energy-flux density is constant. We have a curve which also enters a region of "diminishing returns" for increase of energy-flux density, if capital intensity is constant. We have a different curve for the case that both are increased in parallel. The interesting curves are those which involve the notions of capital intensity and energy-flux density each increasing, but at different rates. Of these, the most interesting are those in which the relative rate of increase of each varies in a linear or non-linear way, in which the rates of change of relative increase of the two are themselves described by a mathematical function. This function is a function of the level of capital intensity and of energy-flux density.

In other words, in the most interesting cases, it is impossible to advance the capital intensity efficiently without operating simultaneously at some minimal level of energy-flux density. It is impossible to increase the energy-flux density efficiently without operating at some minimal level of capital intensity. This interesting case, is the case encountered in real-life economic processes.

Imagine the hypothetical case, that two heat-powered machines consume the same amount of coal-generated power per hour, but that the operative using one of the two types of heat-powered machines has a higher rate of output than the same kind of operative using the other type. The difference between the two types of machines is a difference in the internal organization of the machines. This difference is Leibniz's definition of the subject matter of *technology* (in French: *polytechnique*).

Physical economy is the study of the indicated types of mathematical functions from the standpoint of *technology*.

In first approximation, technology is defined by the *equivalent quantity of circular action* for the transformation of applied power into work-action by the machine.

As in astronomy, for example, the internal processes of the machine are studied as cycles of changes in direction of applied action, and an inclusive cycle is defined subsuming the lesser cycles. By aid of what Cusa defined as the minimum-maximum principle, the isoperimetric principle, the circular action equivalent to the action performed by the machine is determined. This is the application of the Principle of Least Action to the analysis of the technology of the machine cycle.

This procedure is not adopted because many machines are associated with rotary action; machines are dominated by rotating action because that is required by the physical principle of nature corresponding to Leibniz's Principle of Least Action.

To add the function of the Z axis of our general mathematical function, we must reflect increase of energy-flux density within the interpretation of circular action. This results in a higher order of circular action, *conical-spiral action*. The deeper implications of this become clear after examining this feature of the function from the vantage-point of work on self-similar conical-spiral functions accomplished by Gauss and Riemann.

It is admitted that, except for the writer and his collaborators, no institution in the world today practices economic science as Leibniz defined it; outside the circles of the writer, in no known case does any university treat economic science as Physical Economy, or recognize that Physical Economy and mathematical physics are overlapping, inseparable subject-matters of inquiry. New work in the field of Physical Economy vanished in the aftermath of the 1815 Congress of Vienna. Apart from the cameralist programs established or taken over by Leibniz's influence, the principal center practicing Physical Economy at the beginning of the nineteenth century was the 1794–1815 École Polytechnique under Lazare Carnot and Carnot's former teacher Gaspard Monge. Beginning 1816, with Carnot's exile to Germany, the institution was taken over, and ruined, by Pierre-Simon Laplace (1749–1827), a destruction continued under the influence of Augustin Cauchy (1789–1857).[9]

The application of principles of Physical Economy to

issues of political economy was continued, and fruitfully, after 1815 by such leading spokesmen for the American System of political economy as Friedrich List (1789–1846), Henry C. Carey (1793–1879) and E. Peshine Smith (1814–1882). Carey, together with Henry Clay, was a leader of the Whigs and President Abraham Lincoln's instructor in economics. Carey's friend E. Peshine Smith was, from 1872 onward, advisor to the Meiji Restoration in Japan, assisting in guiding Japan toward an industrialization admired and envied today in many quarters of the world. Thus, their work had major impact upon world history during and after their lifetimes, but they contributed only marginally to the body of knowledge of economic science as developed by Leibniz and his followers from 1671 through 1815. Leibniz's current and method in physical science was otherwise vigorously maintained in some leading institutions in Germany through the deaths of Karl Gauss (1855), Gauss's immediate successor, Lejeune Dirichlet (1859), and the collaborator and successor of both Gauss and Dirichlet, Riemann (1866). Although Dirichlet, a protégé of Alexander von Humboldt, studied with the École Polytechnique in collaboration with Humboldt, and although Humboldt himself was in conspiratorial collaboration with Carnot until the latter's death in 1823, Humboldt's circle at the university in Berlin and their allies around Gauss and Göttingen did not extend their relevant breakthroughs in mathematical physics into the domain of Physical Economy as such. It is remarkable that this writer should have been the first to recognize the appropriateness of Riemann's work for economic science's key unsolved problems, in 1952.

Henry C. Carey was at least somewhat aware of this problem and its significance. Notable to this is Carey's 1872 *The Unity of Law*. Broadly, Carey's objective is the correct one, and numerous of the arguments in the book are conceptions not to be overlooked by any serious student of economics. The unfortunate aspect of the book is that Carey was, at the time, under the influence of misplaced admiration for

Henry C. Carey

Göttingen University's Professor Eugen Dühring,[10] a mayfly celebrity of that period. Under this influence, Carey's references to physical principles adopt the authority of personalities and doctrines directly opposed to the current of Gauss and Riemann. Thus, although Carey correctly insists that thermodynamics be taken into account in economic science, he leans upon the wrong doctrine of thermodynamics.

The writer's own contributions to economic science center around a discovery first effected during 1952. As an outgrowth of a 1948–1952 effort to compose a refutation of the Wiener-Shannon "information theory" doctrine, he was led into study of the 1871–1883 work of Georg Cantor on transfinite orderings. This led the present writer to a fresh, corrected view of Riemann's work of the period 1852–1859.[11] He recognized that Riemann's mathematical physics implicitly solved the problem of measuring the relationship between a quantity of technological progress and consequent increases in the rate of economic growth. Hence, the method developed from this starting-point is named the LaRouche-Riemann method.

Among the students of the writer's classes in economic science have been included numbers of mathematicians and other specialists in mathematical physics and related disciplines. With aid of their collaboration over the period since approximately 1970, a significant elaboration of the originally developed form of the LaRouche-Riemann method's application has been accomplished. This work in economic science has overlapped inseparably work in progress in controlled thermonuclear fusion and kindred frontiers of plasma physics. To that degree, the tradition of Leibniz and the École Polytechnique has been revived.

The importance of such an overlap in activities is illustrated in the following terms.

Let us suppose that in a certain case, we lose 80% of the power-input supplied to a machine or process, in the course of developing applied effort of several orders of magnitude or more of increased energy-flux density. Yet, in some such cases, we accomplish more work-output than could be obtained by applying 100% of the input-power at lower energy-flux densities. We have noted this curious phenomenon above: *the simple conversion of energy into work is a fallacious notion.* The same curious phenomenon is the central feature of living processes, but also confronts us in other aspects of scientific work.

As we shall demonstrate later in this text, economic science considered from the vantage-point of Riemann's mathematical physics obliges us to define *work* and *energy* in a certain way, a way contrary to that popularized by Clausius (1822–1888), Helmholtz (1821–1894), Maxwell (1831–1879), and Boltzmann (1844–1906). For reasons established with certainty by Kepler and Gauss's completion of the relevant features of Kepler's work, the notions of work and energy derived from economic science are necessarily the correct notions, and are congruent with the notions of Riemann's mathematical physics *qua* physics. The economic scientist is therefore obliged to search in the work of physicists and biologists for those kinds of experimental cases in which the subject-matter requires the same immediate notions of *work* and *energy* arising from economics. The principal purpose of such searches is to isolate those aspects of physical processes which, by their nature, are the most fruitful for the advancement of technology.

NOTES

1. After Papin had demonstrated the success of a steam-powered river craft, he went to England carrying the specifications of his design, and soon disappeared. Later, some parodies of Papin's invention appeared as British inventions.

2. Germany was, of course, already a center of mining technology during the fifteenth century. However, the region of Germany in which mining technology was concentrated was plunged back almost to savagery by the 1525–1526 civil war and its brutal aftermath. The ruinous effects of the 1618–1648 Thirty Years War compounded the problems. It was not until after Cardinal Mazarin's 1653 defeat of the Hapsburgs that ruined and depopulated Germany began to recover. The forces rebuilding Germany, including Leibniz himself, looked to France for the science and technology needed. It was during and after Leibniz's adulthood that the great development of Germany as a center of the world's mining technology was established once more.

3. This was the Gilbert who elaborated the basis for the modern knowledge of the Earth's magnetic field (e.g., *De Magnete*, 1600), and was also the discoverer of the phenomenon of the magnetic plasma. He has tended to be much underrated in some circles, since he was not only a factional opponent of the Cecils and Francis Bacon in Queen Elizabeth's immediate circles, but was the chief target of Bacon's later efforts to eradicate

the influence of the scientific method of Cusa, Leonardo da Vinci, Gilbert, Kepler, and others from seventeenth-century Britain.

4. During the seventeenth century, there were numerous efforts to discredit the scientific merit of Kepler's work, by the Jesuit Robert Fludd, by Galileo Galilei, by René Descartes, and the circles of William Petty's London Royal Society. However, these criticisms were devastatingly refuted by Gauss's discovery that Kepler had accurately predicted the harmonic orbital values for the asteriod Pallas, and Gauss's solution to the determination of elliptic functions. Kepler stands today as the first to provide a comprehensive body of mathematical laws for determining action within the universe, and is thus the founder of modern mathematical physics.

5. Riemann was a student of Professor Jacob Steiner, the author of synthetic geometry curricula for secondary schools. From archives in Italy, the writer's collaborators gained copies of notes by the Italian mathematician Enrico Betti (1823–1892) on conversations with Riemann during the latter's exile in Italy. Riemann's influence inspired Betti and Betti's circle of allies, producing the great mathematical physics school in that country. In these notes, Riemann stresses the importance of educating future scientists with aid of a rigorous training in the work of Steiner (1796–1863) on synthetic geometry.

6. Since the extant English translations of Plato's *Timaeus* dialogue, Benjamin Jowett's most emphatically, were deliberately falsified wherever Jowett strongly objected to Plato's conceptions, the writer commissioned a new translation in 1978. Until the collection of manuscripts brought to Cosimo de Medici from Greece during the fifteenth century, the *Timaeus* was the only well-studied work of Plato's in Western Europe; it has a central importance, together with the *Critias* and the *Laws*, in implicitly summing up Plato's scientific knowledge. It is the *Timaeus,* among Plato's dialogues, which had a central position in the attention of all of the founders of modern European physical science.

7. Later in this text, the reasons why the Golden Section appears in certain classes of processes will be made clear; *there is nothing*

magical in numbers. Once the reason for the Golden Section's appearance is understood, it is impossible to attempt to superimpose "properties" upon this ratio or any other number.

8. Although National Income Accounting is necessary for the practice of economic science, its function is gathering of data for economic scientists' uses, but it is not itself a part of economic science. That is to say, it is incompetence to attempt to adduce laws of economic processes from the data of National Income Accounting as such.

9. The case of the plagiarized paper of Niels Abel (1802–1829) by Cauchy is typical of Cauchy. Abel had submitted a paper to A. M. Legendre (1752–1833). Legendre was the leading mathematician of France at the time (*Treatise on Elliptic Functions*), and predecessor of and direct influence upon Abel, Riemann and others then and slightly later. Cauchy intercepted Abel's paper and hid it, producing similar conceptions meanwhile as his own work, while denying any knowledge of the whereabouts of Abel's work. Later, after Cauchy's death, the missing paper turned up neatly filed in Cauchy's files.

10. This is the Professor Eugen Dühring who was saved from well-earned obscurity by the pen of Friedrich Engels. On Engels, *cf.* Anton Chaitkin, *Treason in America,* New York, 1984. Engels was a British agent of Lord Palmerston's faction, who served periodically as the controller of British intelligence asset Karl Marx, sharing this function with such British officials as the famous David Urquhart and others. The reason for Engels' attack on the poor Dühring was Dühring's international political connections, an issue which Engels omits to confide to readers of his somewhat celebrated *Anti-Dühring* polemic. Lord Palmerston shared control over Giuseppe Mazzini's Young Europe conspiracy; Marx was a tool of Mazzini's until Mazzini's controllers ordered Marx dumped, about 1869. After Marx was dead, Engels posthumously constructed a legend of his, Engels', friendship with Marx which was considerably exaggerated, to say the least. Thus, wherever Marxists foregather, the name of Professor Eugen Dühring is celebrated as the target of Engels' *ex cathedra* discourse on method. The point remains: Carey was duped by Dühring, although never by Engels.

11. Until the close of the 1970s, this writer and his associates had virtually no knowledge of Riemann's work beyond approximately 1859. The problem was that Riemann was slowly dying of a congenital tuberculosis which appears to have killed many members of his family at an early age. In addition to suffering the difficulties of an "inquisition" conduited through the circles of Clausius, Helmholtz, et al. (since no later than 1857), Riemann's deteriorating condition virtually deprived him of use of his hands for writing from rather early during the 1860s; it was not until a research project into the Riemann archive, begun about 1978, led Uwe Parpart-Henke into searching the Betti archives in Italy, that our knowledge of Riemann's thinking during the 1860–1866 period was at least significantly improved.

The dating, 1852–1859, is defined as follows. Riemann's habilitation dissertation ("On The Hypotheses Which Underlie Geometry"), of publication date 1854, and actually delivered during 1853, was one of three drafted dissertations Riemann had prepared for the 1853 habilitation, under his patron Gauss. The other two are available in the archive of unpublished works, and are papers of utmost importance in the internal history of science, despite the scant knowledge of those papers as such.

On the basis of that evidence, we date the "Riemann" of his mathematical physics from the period of writing of these three prospective habilitation dissertations. The date 1859 identifies the issuance of the treatise "On the Propagation of Plane Air Waves of Finite Magnitude," and a point at which the bulk of Riemann's work on electrodynamics had been completed. (1861 notes from Riemann's Göttingen Lectures on electrodynamics, published by Karl Hattendorf, 1875). Some might choose the date of the earlier dissertation (1851), rather than the preparation of the habilitation dissertation; the quibble is not worth exertion; that is the gist of our indication of the 1852–1859 period.

CHAPTER 2

Potential Relative Population-Density

As Henry Carey rightly insisted,[1] the true measure of the *value* of human productive activity is the increase of *the economy of labor*, through aid of technological progress ("labor-saving"). This was also the fundamental principle for U.S. Treasury Secretary Alexander Hamilton, in his December 1791 "On The Subject of Manufactures." It is the principle shared among all of the leading figures of the American System of political economy, as it was for Leibniz. It is the only definition of *economic value* implicitly consistent with the cited injunctions to mankind in the Book of Genesis.

Why this is necessarily, conclusively proven to be the case, we shall show in due course as we progress in this text. For the present moment, it is sufficient to note that without *economy of labor*, there can be no growth in the per capita output, or consumption, of society, no economic progress. Without economic progress, through technological progress in the *economy of labor*, mankind would still be in the so-called hunting-and-gathering phase of existence.

In that form of existence, the average habitable land area required to sustain the life of an average person is approximately ten square kilometers. This indicates an estimated maximum population of our planet, of approximately ten million individuals.[2] The life-expectancy of the person in such a mode of existence is significantly below twenty years of age: signifying that the majority of the population must be composed of pre-adolescent children.

Admittedly, the indigenous population the colonists

encountered in North America are usually classed by anthropologists as "hunters and gatherers" in the main, but even the best approximation of a hunting-and-gathering culture, the "Digger Indians," are proven to have degenerated to that condition from a relatively higher level of culture. Most of the Indian cultures were degenerated offshoots of relatively advanced cultures in the Americas prior to 1000 B.C., and some of the Indian cultures were also admixtures with colonies from Scandinavia, Ireland, and Portuguese fisherman's colonies, some of these European colonies established hundreds of years before Christopher Columbus used the kinds of maps assembled at Florence in A.D. 1439, to guide him along the same route which Homer's *Odyssey* describes as used by the legendary Ulysses in his trip (circa 1000 B.C.) into the Caribbean regions.[3]

In a "true" hunting-and-gathering culture,[4] one which did not preserve some of the technologies of a more advanced level of culture into its degenerated state, the human condition would compare poorly with that of the stronger and faster baboon. Without the principle of progress in the *economy of labor,* the human population today would be composed of approximately ten million persons, or less, existing in such a miserable condition.

For the moment, until later in this text, we overlook the proof that mankind *today* could not continue to exist without continued technological progress. For the moment, we limit ourselves to the more obvious evidence, that human progress, in all respects, is impossible without continuing improvement of the economy of labor through the mediation of technological progress.

It is readily comprehended, that the increase of man's power over nature is most easily measured as a decrease of the habitable land area required to sustain an average person. This measures the economy of labor in a most effective way; this measure can be applied to each and all forms of society without regard to the wide assortment of distinctions in internal culture and structure among societies in general.

The name for this measurement is, in first approximation, *population-density*. Given, a society's level of technology in practice, how many persons can be sustained, per square kilometer, solely by means of the labor of that society's population?

However, before we proceed to measure, we must make certain adjustments in our definition of population-density. First, land varies in quality for human habitation. This variability is threefold. Relative to any technological level of culture, various pieces of land vary in quality of suitability and fertility for human habitation and other use. However, human habitation does not leave land in a permanently fixed condition. The quality of habitability and other use is worsened by effects of depletion; the quality is improved by means including irrigation, fertilization, and so forth. Finally, a change in technology is a change in the qualities of land most suitable for human use. These three kinds of interacting variability of quality of land must be taken into account in comparing the "habitability" of one square kilometer of land with another. These three considerations define the variable quality of land as *relative* value of a square kilometer.

Instead of measuring simple square kilometers, we must measure *relative square kilometers*. We must measure, therefore, *relative population-density*.

Second, there is usually a significant difference between the size of population which could be supported with existing levels of technology, and the current size of the population. It is the former which we must measure in comparing different levels of technological development of cultures. We must measure the *potential* population, defined in this way.

We must measure the *potential relative population-density*. This is the rough measure of the superiority of one level of culture over another. This is the measure of *economic progress;* it is the measure of *economy of labor.*

We must go one step further. For reasons to be shown as we proceed in this text, the quantity we must measure is the *rate of increase* of potential relative population-density.

This measures the *rate of economy of labor,* the rate at which the productive powers of labor are being increased. For reasons we shall demonstrate in due course, this is the only scientific basis for measuring *economic value.* The measure of *economic value* is *the rate of increase of potential relative population-density, relative to the existing level of potential relative population-density.*

In mathematical terms, such a measurement of economic value has a precise meaning in the language of functions of a complex variable. This is best defined and understood by comprehending the general theory of functions of a complex variable from the same standpoint Karl Gauss elaborated the generation of elliptic functions.

Gauss accomplished this by working from the standpoint of synthetic geometry: the synthetic geometry of self-similar conical-spiral constructions. From this geometrical vantage-point, the ontological significance of functions of a complex variable can be mastered by a literate secondary-school pupil, and all the superstitious mystification often attached to the term "imaginary numbers" evaporates. The chief problems left unsolved by Gauss, and also by Legendre's, Abel's, and Karl Jacobi's (1804–1851) work on elliptic functions, were implicitly solved by what Bernhard Riemann caused to be celebrated under the name "Dirichlet's Principle." By applying Dirichlet's Principle to the work of Gauss, Legendre, et al., Riemann achieved a general form of solution for mastery of such conceptions. Hence the LaRouche-Riemann method, the attachment of Riemann's method to the economic discoveries of LaRouche.

Admittedly, the attempt to master these matters from the standpoint of a deductive algebra based on axiomatic arithmetic is laborious and frightening even among many professional mathematicians. If the proper, synthetic-geometrical approach is employed instead, the mystification drops away to the extent that a secondary-school pupil could master the essentials. Therefore, the reader of this text should not

It can be demonstrated that progress is a necessity. Above: Ben Franklin bridge between Camden, New Jersey, and Philadelphia.

be affrighted by forewarning of the nature of the conceptions toward which we are working.

No intelligent layman could honestly argue that such progress is not advantageous. It should be clear, that to attempt to return to a hunting-and-gathering mode of existence, as some among the more radical of today's "environmentalists" demand, would oblige us to wipe out about four and a half billion of the Earth's present level of population: the most savage mass murder in known history. If this return to a lower technological level of culture were attempted, the genocide so caused would be accomplished chiefly through interrelated eruptions of famine and epidemic, the most efficient modes of mass murder ever devised.

Such mass murder (*genocide,* according to the doctrine presented by U.S. Justice Robert Jackson at the Nuremberg Trials) could be accomplished to a large degree simply by adopting the policy of "post-industrial society" globally for a span of from four to five decades. The fall in productivity of labor, measured in physical-goods output, would lower the potential relative population-density way below existing levels of population. After about fifty years of such policy of practice, the potential would fall to the vicinity of world population levels of about one billion. It is not improbable that the flowering of the immunological potentials of populations most affected would cause large-scale eruptions of both old and new varieties of epidemics and pandemics to a degree sufficient to eradicate the human species entirely from this planet. There is not much good to be said for "environmentalism" as currently preached.

Putting to one side the criminal proposals to lower the technological level of culture, the question remains whether technological progress might not be halted at present levels of development? In other words, *is continued technological progress indispensable for continued human existence, as well as simply advantageous?* We shall come shortly to the point in our text at which a preliminary, and more or less conclusive "Yes" is proven to be the answer to the question: technological progress is indispensable for continuing human existence on this planet. At later stages of the text, the same proof will be explored from a more advanced standpoint.

We turn now to the question of applying the notion of potential relative population-density to existing economies. We begin with an approximation which is rough in texture, but sound in principle. We shall thus bring some leading conceptions of applied economic science to light, and move on from that point, to later examination of the same conceptions in a more rigorous and profound way.

For preliminary examination of any economy, treat any large national economy as if all of its activities were those of a consolidated agro-industrial firm. The operatives employed either in producing agricultural and industrial output, or in constructing, maintaining, and operating basic economic infrastructure essential to agricultural and industrial production of physical goods, should be treated as *productive labor.* All other categories of either employment or unemployment fall into the categories of *overhead expenses* of the consolidated agro-industrial enterprise. Overhead expenses include administration, services, selling costs, and expenses, and various forms of waste including unemployment.

The cycle of production of physical-goods output of the consolidated agro-industrial enterprise, we trace most usefully backwards: from final commodities, to intermediate commodities, to production of raw materials. Final commodities are assorted into two principal "market-baskets": capital-goods "market-baskets" and household-consumption-goods "market-baskets." We trace, backwards, the flow of intermediate commodities and raw materials into each of the two sets of "market-baskets." We subdivide the "market-baskets" into two general subcategories for each:

a) Capital goods consumed for production of physical-goods-output plus construction, maintenance, and operation of basic economic infrastructure.
b) Capital goods consumed as required items of overhead-expense activities.
c) Consumer goods required by households of employed operatives.
d) Consumer goods required by households whose employment falls in the categories of overhead expense.

We measure these market-baskets in per capita terms: a) per capita for population as a whole; b) per capita for labor force as a whole; c) per capita for the operatives' component of the labor force as a whole. We define these per capita measurements in terms of consumption and also in terms of production of the components of the market-baskets. This might be described as *a method for measuring the input-output relations within a self-contained economic process as a whole.*

This approach is sufficient to explore the dangers to society inherent in a "zero-technological-growth" policy.

At any level of technology, certain aspects of man-altered nature are the principal "natural resources" upon which raw-materials production depends. In such a case, at any given point, the production of the raw materials required for production to fill the market-baskets to needed levels requires the allotment of an estimated percentile of the total labor force to raw-materials production. We should also observe that this allotment must be measured also as a percentile of the operatives component of the total labor force.

If the spectrum of the varieties of natural resources required by such a technological culture is depleted, the society is obliged to employ relatively poorer and less accessible varieties of these resources. This increases the labor cost per unit of raw materials produced. The percentile of the labor force required for raw-materials production is increased. In consequence, less production occurs as other aspects of production are constricted; in consequence the content of market-baskets is reduced. *This represents a lowering of the potential relative population-density.*

If this lowering of the potential falls below the existing levels of population, the society itself enters a collapse-spiral, not unlike the collapse of Italy under the rule of Rome, caused by a combination of zero-technological-growth policies for the economy, including the displacement of productive Italian free farmers by marginally productive slave labor of the aristocratic estates. Italy was gradually depopulated as a result of this process, one of the leading causes of the political ferment associated with the Flaminian reforms and the abortive Gracchian insurgencies. The Roman Empire subsisted thereafter on the basis of tribute (including grain imports) brought into Italy by subjugation of other peoples. As large tracts of conquered territory declined in a manner similar to Italy, for the same reasons of policy, the Roman Empire collapsed internally. In modern times, the rate of collapse induced by such policies of practice is greatly accelerated, relative to the Roman case, because the relative reliance on technology to maintain present population levels is much greater. There are other factors, which it would be a digression to list at this point; the general point is made sufficiently clear as the matter stands.

These effects of depletion are resisted, or even successfully superseded, by technological progress. There are two aspects to this effect of technological progress. First, simply, increase of the productive powers of labor compensates for the rise in average cost of the market-basket. Economy of labor permits the same amount of work to be accomplished with less human effort, with a smaller allotment of the labor force to the average category of production of physical goods. If technological progress is sufficiently rapid, the economy will grow successfully despite depletion of part of the spectrum of required natural resources. Similarly, the allotment of some of the labor-savings obtained through technological progress to improvements of infrastructure, raises the relative quality of land for habitation and other use by society: irrigation, transportation, and so forth.

Second, what might be fairly labeled "technological revolutions" change the spectrum of required natural resources. The "agricultural revolution" is an exemplary case. The use of animal power, the use of water power, wind power, the industrial revolution based on the heat-powered machine is another; the electricity revolution is another. By limiting the growth of plant life on areas of land to varieties of use to mankind, and by improving the varieties of plants grown, the finite amount of solar radiation striking the land (about 0.2 kilowatts per square meter) is concentrated to man's benefit; the relative quality of land is greatly increased; the potential relative population density is greatly increased. Today, the chief parameters of a successful technological revolution are both cheapening the cost of producing and delivering usable energy supplies and, at the same time, increasing the

Civilization advanced and expanded as the agricultural revolution took hold. In the Arab world, it began in the seventh century A.D.

energy-flux density and the coherence of those energy supplies; such methods make very poor-grade ore as cheap to employ as was earlier the case only with very high-grade ore, for example.

On such grounds, we are able to prove that technological progress is not merely advantageous, but is also indispensable to continued human existence. *Only societies whose cultures commit them to successful technological progress, as a policy of practice, are qualified to survive and to prosper.* Indeed, only such societies are *morally* qualified to survive, as the society based on the law and culture of Rome was not.

As mankind progresses in technology of practice, the amount of usable energy used by society increases *both* per capita and per square kilometer. In broad terms, we may reduce this to the form of a single mathematical function, by correlating energy per square kilometer with potential relative population density: a function of *rising (usable) energy per square kilometer as the potential relative population-density increases.* This is not yet an exact function, but is a useful approximation of the required function.

As we have implied just above, historically, the increase of usable energy-throughput is roughly divided into two general phases. In the first phase, the emphasis is upon increasing the effective capture of solar energy. The agricultural revolution, the use of water power, and the use of windmill power, are examples of this indirect use of energy sources of solar radiation (chiefly). The second phase is a gradual shift of emphasis toward use of non-solar sources: fossil fuels, fission energy, and controlled thermonuclear fusion.

Solar energy is a very limited, ultimately very poor source of energy at present levels of potential relative population-density. We have noted that the average solar radiation striking the Earth's surface is a mere 0.2 kilowatts per square meter. Tables 1 and 2 on page 34 were compiled by the Fusion Energy Foundation during 1979: Although the prices in Table 2 are obviously outdated, the relative values of those prices are nonetheless indicative today.

It is to be emphasized, that water power, wind power, and plant and animal energy sources are forms of capture of solar radiation. That available at the Earth's surface, we have stressed, is 0.2 kilowatts per square meter. At 8 million kilometers from the Sun, the energy-flux density rises only to 1.4 kilowatts per square meter. As burnable energy captured in biomass, the yield from capture of solar energy by plant life

Table 1
ENERGY-FLUX DENSITIES COMPARED

Energy Source	Energy-Flux Densities in Kilowatts/Square Meter
Solar Energy (surface of Earth)	0.0002
Fossil Fuels	10,000
Fission Energy	70,000
Fusion Energy (A.D. 2000)	70,000
Fusion Energy (21st Century)	10^{15}

Table 2
COSTS OF ENERGY

Source	Cost $/Megawatt-hour	Capital Investment Billion $/gigawatt
Oil	45.7	0.94
Coal	31.7	0.97
Coal Gas	55.7	1.67
Light-Water Fission	28.5	1.16
Fast Breeder	33.9	1.43
Fusion (A.D. 2000)	45.2	1.92
Solar Collector	490.0	20.90
Solar Cells	680.0	28.90

is merely 0.0002 kilowatts per square meter of the land from which this plant life is obtained.

The agricultural revolution was a great development, an indispensable development for all of human culture, but, in the broad view of the matter, it is narrowly limited in potential if we rely upon solar radiation alone, and, on the appropriate time scale, biomass has a very short historical life as a source of heat power. In the development of plants as food sources, the limitations associated with that aspect of the matter are illustrated by the point that our best present performance in improving strains of grains permits only 50% of the total plant weight to be usable grain; without greatly

In the 20th and 21st centuries, water-management systems requiring significant energy inputs are a prerequisite for sufficient improvement of land. Above: the Tarbela dam system in Pakistan.

increasing the plant weight per hectare, we cannot much improve the quantity of grain yield per hectare beyond best varieties today. To obtain the quality of animal protein necessary for healthy development of young persons, and to sustain high immunological potentials, and so forth, we must lose part of the total plant life production in converting such agricultural product to livestock food output. Only the treatment of soils with chemical fertilizers, trace-element maintenance, pesticides, and so forth, permits us to improve plant varieties for significantly higher yields than are possible with merely solar radiation plus "natural fertilizers." Only by radical improvements in land, including extensive water-management systems which require significant energy inputs at some point in the process, can we obtain high relative values of agricultural land per square kilometer more generally.

With fossil fuels, and the "chemistry revolution" of the eighteenth and nineteenth centuries made possible and provoked by use of fossil fuels for the industrial revolution, mankind made a large step toward breaking out of the constraints of solar radiation sources. Yet, fossil fuels have a limited historical life for mankind's general use. Coal is sedimentary residue of plant life, and finite in extent on that account. Petroleum and natural gas, combined, are not strictly "fossil fuels" in the same sense as coal is; petroleum and natural gas are produced "naturally" in whatever part of our planet the proper chemical preconditions exist, and a "reducing," as opposed to "oxidizing" environment prevails. No doubt, the Earth today is continuously producing new supplies of petroleum and natural gas deep in the planet's mantle. Nonetheless, in the long term, this, too, is a limited resource for mankind. The same general observation applies to fission-energy potential on Earth, at least insofar as we rely upon fissionable materials extracted from ores.

With controlled thermonuclear fusion, we escape such limitations. Hydrogen is abundant in the universe, and obtaining the deuterium isotope from hydrogen-isotope mixtures available on Earth and elsewhere is well established. Immediately, fusion fuel is almost unlimited relative to other sources of energy production on Earth, and, as technology advances the fuel supply will become totally unlimited to all foreseeable practical purposes for millennia and longer to come. At very, very high energy-flux densities available within the scope of development of controlled thermonuclear fusion, a properly organized form of such an ultra-high energy-flux density plasma can be used to manufacture fuels for ordinary fusion processes from ordinary hydrogen, for example. Thus, as we verge now on economic breakthroughs in production of net energy output from controlled thermonuclear fusion's "first-generation" prototypes, we are at the brink of unlimited "artificial energy" supplies.

The proposal to rely upon "renewable energy" resources, promoted by former Energy Secretary James R. Schlesinger and many others of that faction, is clearly suicidal policy. We have indicated adequately the problem of use of "biomass" as a substitute for nuclear energy and fossil fuels. In the case of the solar collector, or solar cell, the amount of energy consumed by society in producing such devices exceeds the total energy collected over the useful life of the device. In other words, the "energy payback" to society for relying upon such devices is *negative*.

Among the leading points illustrated by Table 2, there is a connection between the efficiency of heat sources and the temperature (or equivalent) level at which the energy source operates. The memory of Sadi Carnot (1796–1832) is evoked by this table. As long as one adheres to the "caloric theory of percussive heat," Carnot's famous formulation appears to account for the fact that more costly processes of heat generation can compete with less costly ones if the more costly operate at a sufficiently greater energy-flux density than the less costly. However, Sadi Carnot himself was never at ease with the "caloric" theory, and employed its assumptions merely as a convenience at the time he wrote his 1824 treatise. The conclusive refutation of the "statistical theory of heat" was later accomplished by Riemann, in his 1859 "On The Propagation of Plane Air Waves of Finite Magnitude," one of the most important of the sources employed by the LaRouche-Riemann method. Lord Rayleigh (1843–1919), writing during the 1890s, was among those who emphasized that if Riemann's 1859 treatise were proven sound, the entirety of statistical gas theory would be overturned. The later work of German scientists proved Riemann's treatise experimentally. Professor Erwin Schrödinger (1887–1961) on the internal geometry of the electron was also indebted to this treatise of Riemann's. There is something much deeper behind the results shown in Table 2 than could ever be adduced within the bounds of the caloric theory of heat.

This bears upon that curious phenomenon to which

we referred earlier in the text: the instance in which *a mere portion of the total power supplied to a process, by virtue of that portion's being raised to a sufficiently high energy-flux density, accomplishes more work than the entire power supplied, if the latter is applied at significantly lower energy-flux densities.*

In part, this curious phenomenon includes situations in which a chemical reaction, for example, cannot occur unless the reaction is energized at a certain minimal energy-flux density. There are numerous analogous instances, of course. Such examples bear upon the point to be developed later in this text, but the point to be developed goes deeper than those examples tend to imply.

NOTES

1. *Unity of Law, passim.*
2. Estimates compiled from research by Uwe Parpart-Henke.
3. A rough reconstruction of this voyage from the description supplied in the *Odyssey* was accomplished in 1978 by classical Greek scholars. The specifications would require a craft like the Viking long-ships, which did in fact proliferate in the Mediterranean during the second millennium B.C. The "spirit of the ship" in the account strongly suggests a magnetic compass, actually not an unlikely technology during that period—for reasons too detailed to be reported here.
4. The earliest imputable historical account of a truly primitive hunting-and-gathering culture appears in the account of the Atlas people, as reported in Diodorus Siculus (1st century B.C. Roman historian). The Atlas people, inhabitants of the fertile region of modern Morocco near the Strait of Gilbraltar, insist that their ancient forebears were a crude hunting-and-gathering culture at the time an urban center was established by a maritime culture which taught the indigenous population agriculture. This is the

"Atlantis" culture of Plato's dialogues. The dynastic names of this culture correspond to the pre-dynastic names of Egypt's earliest period. What are often classified as "hunting-and-gathering" cultures among anthropologists are not strictly "primitive" cultures, but the products of the collapse and degeneration of a relatively higher level of culture.

CHAPTER 3

The Thermodynamics of Political Economy

Under assorted academic and other auspices, one is frequently confronted by references to one or more of three putative "Laws of Thermodynamics." Except for the lazy fellows who never challenge the authenticity of assertions offered by textbooks, dictionaries, and encyclopedias, a reasonable amount of inquiry into the source of these "laws" discloses that the notion of "law" employed is a legislative, not scientific quality. They represent the arbitrary, factional superimposition of Aristotle's notion of energy *(energeia)* upon practiced mathematical physics during the second half of the nineteenth century, by such figures as Clausius, Helmholtz, Maxwell, and the unfortunate Boltzmann.[1] The three "Laws of Thermodynamics" are not only arbitrary; they had been proven false, and conclusively so, by Johannes Kepler, centuries before their introduction.

Although identification of the proofs involved belongs to a later stage of the present text, we report the fact of the matter here to forewarn the reader of the provisional quality of the illustrative discussion into which we are plunging at this point. As in the case of Sadi Carnot, the initial description of the phenomenon of heat employs the measurement of heat in terms of the simple arithmetic temperature scale. In first approximation, we measure heat as a quantity of heat defined by the work required to raise the temperature one degree on the Centigrade or Fahrenheit scale. For sake of consistency, we then measure the conversion of heat into work as the using-up of a quantity of heat implicitly measured by a drop

41

in the temperature of the heat applied. There is nothing wrong in employing this set of assumptions merely for the purpose of initial description of phenomena, provided that we, more or less as Sadi Carnot was, are suspicious of those assumptions. The assumptions are useful for first approximation, but are provably false if carried beyond the scope of such initial approximations. In this section of the text, we limit our attention to matters of initial approximation.

Our initial approximation now proceeds.

Divide the total energy-throughput into two principal subcategories. The portion of the energy-throughput which the process itself must appear to consume to avoid "running down" is termed the *energy of the system*. The term "running down" was brought into usage by Isaac Newton and the discussion of Newton's point in the Leibniz-Clarke correspondence: the image employed is the "running down" of the mainspring of a simple mechanical timepiece. This is the historical root of the definition of *entropy* in ordinary mechanics. The *energy of the system* is considered to include the loss of power to accomplish work associated with friction, waste heat, and so forth. If any portion of the energy-throughput remains after the deduction of required *energy of the system,* the remaining portion is named *free energy*.

Let us imagine, for purposes of initial approximation, that economic processes are of the form of the self-contained, consolidated agro-industrial enterprise described earlier in this text. The kind of thermodynamic process we must imagine, to examine the consolidated agro-industrial enterprise thermodynamically, is *a closed thermodynamic process.* All of the sources and applications of energy are contained within the process examined.

In such a case, the *energy of the system* corresponds to the costs and expenses of producing the total physical goods and related output, and the *free energy* is the net operating profit of the enterprise as a whole. The mathematical functions required are obtained by examining the effects of the re-investment of the free energy (net operating profit) as added energy of the system.

The characteristic effect *selected* as measure of the performance of this mathematical function is *economy of labor,* as this was defined in earlier portions of this text. The apparent effect of re-investment of free energy to increase the energy of the system, is to increase the costs of the economy per capita, which might appear to be directly opposite to the result required. In a successful economy, it appears that a directly opposite net result occurs: the social costs of producing a "constant-content market basket" are reduced: economy of labor. To uncover the fallacy embedded within such a paradox, we are led to recognized that there is a "mixing of apples and oranges" in our counting procedure. Yes, the energy of the system does increase, but the cost of supplying this energy, as cost of labor, is reduced. There is an increase of the energy cost of the per capita activities of labor, but the labor cost of producing this energy is reduced sufficient to lower the average cost of per capita labor. This is the result corresponding to the characteristic effect selected for defining our mathematical function.

We now restate this paradox in terms of changes of value of the ratio of free energy to energy of the system. If the quantity of energy-throughput were constant over successive cycles of a thermodynamically described economic process, then the increase of per capita energy of the system, by converting "re-invested" free energy into added energy of the system, must cause the ratio of free energy to energy of the system to fall.[2] Then, as the mathematical function (economic process) were extended over time, the ratio must converge upon zero. If we include the effects of depletion of natural resources within the closed thermodynamic system, the ratio must become negative over time; the economic (thermodynamic) process must collapse.

In the case of the closed thermodynamic process, the fact that the ratio of free energy to energy of the system falls in such a fashion signifies that the process corresponding to such a mathematical function is characteristically *entropic:* the mainspring is winding down. Taking human existence as a whole, the increase of potential relative population-density proves that the desired, anti-entropic result actually exists in economic processes. Increase of the potential relative population-density corresponds to a mathematical function characterized by *negative entropy, negentropy.* This is also the characteristic of living processes, including the existence of the human species.

If we accept the implicit assumptions of the caloric theory of heat, the fact that human existence is negentropic implies that society's continued existence requires mankind to draw down the energy supplies of our environment. This is one among the rationalizations employed by the neo-Malthusian Club of Rome and its sympathizers. "Yes," the better-informed among such circles argue, "perhaps living systems, and perhaps even successful economies, have been negentropic until the present time. The problem is, that we are drawing down the finite supplies of energy from our environment at such a rate that we cannot continue to proceed negentropically."

Earlier, as in the case of the Club of Rome's 1972 *Limits To Growth,* MIT's Dennis Meadows and Jay Forrester argued that economies were intrinsically entropic. Their argument to this effect was accomplished chiefly by using the Leontieff model of input-output relations, the model employed to construct the present U.S. system of National Income Accounting, the same system employed by the United Nations and most nations, too, for measuring the Gross Domestic Product of national economies. Such prevailing methods of National Income Accounting are fundamentally fallacious in many crucial points; the most important of these fallacies in the case of the *Limits to Growth,* is the use of what is called today systems analysis, systems of linear equations, to describe the input-output relations within an economic process. Such use of linear equations asserts arbitrarily that technological progress has abruptly and totally ceased at the moment such systems of linear statements are inserted into the computer. It should be noted also, that Meadows and Forrester rather arbitrarily added to their calculations an estimate of the scale of natural-resources data which was not merely pessimistically low, but fraudulently so. Of these two principal frauds in the work of Meadows and Forrester, the more fundamental was the employment of systems of linear inequalities, systems analysis.

Worse, this fraudulent book was used as a benchmark for the argument that technological progress must be halted. Having asserted implicitly that technological progress does not occur, by employment of systems analysis, it was then argued that this non-occurring technological progress must be stopped from occurring. Having proven, in fact, that the cessation of technological progress leads to a global catastrophe, in *Limits to Growth,* they concluded from this that technological progress must cease. This is analogous to the syllogism, that since cessation of eating causes people to die, people must cease eating. Perhaps, to Meadows, Forrester, and their admirers, the death of the human species were to be preferred to admitting the intrinsic incompetence of systems analysis.

The arguments of the writer and his associates to this effect prompted the leading neo-Malthusians, including leading policy-makers for the Club of Rome, to alter the appearance of their argument.[3] The writer's widely circulated published work on the subject of increase of potential relative population-density embarrassed the policy-makers of the Club of Rome to the effect that they shifted away from the Meadows-Forrester doctrine of *Limits To Growth,* to a simple parody of the eighteenth-century Physiocrats; they insisted that the "carrying capacity" of habitable land was being exceeded at present levels of population. They argued simply, that the universe as a whole is governed by a Law of Entropy, and that man's continued existence was accelerating the rate at which the universe is being urged to its inevitable *Götterdämmerung* of "heat-death." In other words, man's attempt to maintain present levels of population or increase them, by means of technological progress, is accelerating the rate at which mankind draws down the finite energy supplies of his environment; mankind is already at or past the threshhold of consuming energy at a higher rate than the environment supplies. Hence, since we are to accept the report that we are running down short supplies of wood, petroleum, and coal, we must shut down the nuclear energy plants, and postpone indefinitely expenditures leading to development of commercial fusion energy production. The neo-Malthusians are irrational, but consistently and morbidly so.

It ought to be sufficiently clear, that insofar as the indicated arguments of the neo-Malthusians might lay some claim to the authority of science, their arguments rely entirely upon the putative three laws of thermodynamics. We have reported at the outset of this section, that those three laws were arbitrarily superimposed upon thermodynamics beginning approximately 1850.

Formally, the history of the matter is that Sadi Carnot's 1824 work was appropriated for reworking by Rudolf Clausius. In 1850 Clausius laid down what became known to the present day as the Second Law of Thermodynamics. To complement this formulation of the Second Law, the addition of the First and Third Laws of Thermodynamics was required to explain away the obvious fallacies of the Second Law. The overlapping efforts of Clausius, Helmholtz, Maxwell, and Boltzmann established these concoctions as putatively awesome laws. Actually, the basis for these constructions was the doctrine of, principally Laplace and also Laplace's student and successor, Cauchy, earlier during the century. Clausius, Helmholtz, Maxwell, and Boltzmann, principally, working within a framework established by Laplace and Cauchy, established their peculiar doctrine of "black-body radiation" and the "statistical theory of [percussive] heat" which has perplexed science to the present day—a perplexity which has visibly reigned since the suicide of the despondent Boltzmann at the Torre i Tasso (Thurn und Taxis) shrine at Rilke's Duino Castle.

Implicitly, the Second Law of Thermodynamics was conclusively refuted by the work of Johannes Kepler published at the beginning of the seventeenth century, two centuries before Cauchy's incumbency was imposed upon the École Polytechnique by the 1815 Congress of Vienna. Some of the points bearing upon this have been identified earlier in this text. Now, we identify the bearing of that material upon Kepler's proof.

We noted that Pacioli and Leonardo da Vinci had been the first moderns to report that living processes are distinguished from non-living by self-similar growth congruent with the Golden Section. Kepler later re-emphasized the same distinction. The crucial fact bearing upon the Second Law of Thermodynamics is that all of Kepler's laws of astronomy were derived by a construction premised on the starting point of the Golden Section. Since it was later shown by Gauss that Kepler's laws were uniquely appropriate, and since these laws are subsumed by the Golden Section, the universe as a whole has the same characteristic as living processes: *the universe as a whole is characteristically negentropic.*

The significance of the Golden Section is made clear, without burden of superstition or other mystification, by the work of Gauss on determination of elliptic functions.

Construct a self-similar spiral on the side of a cone. The projected image of this spiral upon the circular base of the cone is a plane spiral whose characteristic is the Golden Section. This characteristic is adduced by cutting the arms of the spiral with radii of the circular base. For example, if the radii are drawn to divide the circular base into twelve equal sectors, the radii divide the length of the arms of the spiral into curved segments which are exactly in proportion to the notes of the well-tempered musical scale (Figure 1).[4]

This illustrates the fact, that the occurrence of the Golden Section as characteristic of a process observed in visible (e.g., Euclidean) space is nothing but the projection upon visible space of images of self-similar conical-spiral action in the *continuous manifold* which is the domain of self-similar conical-spiral action, the "complex domain." This becomes clearer through the following exploration of highlights of such conical functions.[5]

First, if the student will study a self-similar spiral constructed upon the side of a cone, and describes the locus of generation of this spiral algebraically, the student will observe that he has produced the most elementary form of a complex variable, $a + bi$. Continuing from this beginning, the other principal "properties" of conical functions *(complex-variable functions)* appear. At the beginning the student has established an elementary *physical* meaning for the notion of a complex variable. Thus, this established, the student is enabled to locate the physical significance of each of the "properties" adduced by further exploration.

Second, the student should construct a direct line from the apex to circular base of the cone, and also construct the line representing the axis of the cone. At each point the self-similar spiral intersects the direct line from apex to base, cut the volume of the cone with a circular cross-section (Figure 2). The student should then imagine that the volume of the cone is the locus of increase of potential relative population-density, such that each circular cross-section identifies a definite potential relative population-density. This affords a geometric image of the physical significance of *negentropy*. *This geometric construction is the proper mathematical definition of negentropy.* The complex-variable function generating the succession of circular cross-sections symbolizes a function of *increase of potential relative population-density.*

Third, the student should connect the successive circular cross-sections within the cone by diagonal ellipses (Figure 3). This is the starting-point for the comprehension of elliptic functions. The student should observe, next, the difference between the geometric and arithmetic mean values for the movement of the spiral from one of the circular cross-sections to the next. The geometric mean corresponds to the circular cross-section at the point of the spiral at which "half of the time has elapsed" between its leaving the beginning point of one complete rotation around the cone and its arrival at the end of one complete such cycle. The arithmetic mean corresponds to a circular cross-section constructed at the mid-point of the cone's axis lying between the beginning and ending of one complete cycle. The student should determine the relationship of the arithmetic and geometric mean to determining the foci of the elliptical diagonal cut of the volume of the cone for a single cycle. On which focus of the elliptical orbit of the Earth does the Sun lie? What does that mean in terms of the physics of conical functions?

Fourth, the student should construct a plane surface, parallel to the cone's base, passing through the apex of the cone. On this plane surface, the student should project images of the diagonal ellipse and its determined features (Figure 4). The apex of a cone will lie on one focus of the ellipse in the plane, the position of the Sun in relationship to the Earth's orbit.

Fifth, the student should subdivide the volume of one cycle of conical-spiral action at the focal points of the original ellipse, next cutting this subdivision of the volume with a second diagonal ellipse (Figure 5). Repeat this for a third, smaller volume similarly determined (Figure 6). At this point, begin describing the ratios of the characteristic values of the series of ellipses being generated.

Sixth, assume that this iterative, elliptical subdivision of the volume of one cycle ends at some point. This point corresponds to some cross-sectional volume of the cone, and

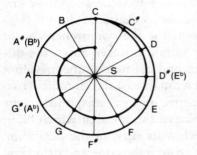

Figure 1
A self-similar, or logarithmic, spiral on a cone, projected down to the cone's base. This spiral halves the distance to the apex (peak of the cone) with each complete rotation. The circle at the base of the cone is divided into twelve sections, and lines are drawn up to the apex. The lengths of those lines between the base (circumference of the circle) and the point at which they intersect the spiral determine the string lengths for each note of the well-tempered octave.

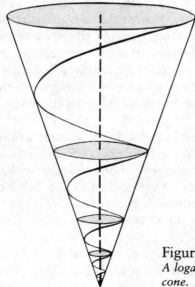

Figure 2
A logarithmic spiral on a cone.

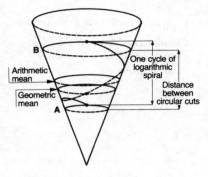

Figure 3

One cyle of a logarithmic circle on a cone defines a conic volume shown in the drawing between circle A and circle B. The geometric mean ($\sqrt{ab}$) of these circles is found at one half-cycle of the spiral. The arithmetic mean (($(a+b)/2$) is found at one-half the distance between the circles A and B.

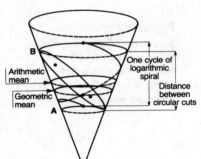

The foci of an elliptical cut between circles A and B are next used to subdivide the volume of the conic section.

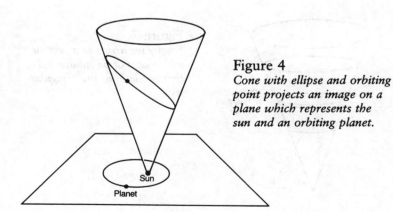

Figure 4

Cone with ellipse and orbiting point projects an image on a plane which represents the sun and an orbiting planet.

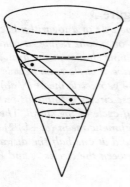

Figure 5
Circular cuts through the foci of the ellipse create a smaller conic volume.

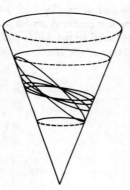

Figure 6
Successive elliptical cuts are made through smaller and smaller conic volumes. (For clarity's sake, the conic volumes are not shown here.)

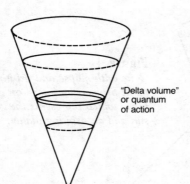

"Delta volume" or quantum of action

Figure 7
Finally we arrive at a volume which cannot be subdivided by this method: the "singularity."

some corresponding segment of the cone's axis (Figure 7). Equate this small interval of volume and line to the smallest value of "delta" in Leibniz's differential calculus. Also designate this as the *singularity* of the negentropic transformation represented by one cycle of the conical spiral.

This conception, so described, defines as a first approximation the implicit topological problem addressed successfully by Dirichlet's Principle. This leads, in turn, directly into Riemann's work, including the mathematical physics program given preliminary statement in Riemann's 1854 habilitation dissertation, the principles of the Riemann Surface, and the principles underlying the cited 1859 dissertation on acoustical shockwaves.

The student should master the indicated topics in mathematics through reference to the relevant primary sources of Gauss, Dirichlet, and Riemann. This should be a required feature of the university curriculum in economic science. Without this grounding, an elaborated mathematical application of economic science is not possible. We limit ourselves here to the most crucial highlights of the matter.

Seventh, the student should explore the case in which the cone is extremely tall and the apex angle of the cone very small. In other words, as our attention shifts away from the apex of the cone, the sideview of the cone approximates a cylinder, and the difference between the arithmetic and geometric mean-values of the self-similar conical spiral becomes correspondingly very small. The circular cross-sections cut at the conclusion of each completed cycle are each nearly close in value to both preceding and succeeding cross-sections. The singularity becomes very small, at whatever limit of iterative elliptic subdivision is assigned. The side-view projection of the self-similar spiral is very close to a sine wave.

Even the student who has not progressed beyond the construction exercises indicated here thus far is able to pause and reflect upon the physical equivalence of self-similar conical-spiral functions to logarithmic, and trigonometric func-

Plato   Nicolaus of Cusa

tions, and the subsumed determination of the transcendental
numbers e and π *(pi)*. Synthetic geometry is a much more
pleasant way to comprehend mathematics than the pathway
defined by the starting-point of an axiomatic arithmetic. The
superstition and other mystification intrinsic to both axiomatic arithmetic and algebras consistent with axiomatic arithmetic, are happily avoided.

At this instant, we register two points to be made clear
as we proceed. The definition of *work* in the LaRouche-Riemann method of economic science is the image of *a negentropic self-similar conical-spiral function*. The definition of
energy, as distinct from *work,* in the LaRouche-Riemann
method, is *a self-similar cylindrical-spiral function*.

To concentrate on the *physical* significance of such
functions of a complex variable, we refer to the problem first
known to have been defined by Plato. Plato insisted that the

visible world has a different appearance than the real world, in the same broad sense of the matter as the distorted shadows projected upon the walls of a dark cave by firelight. St. Paul writes that we see as if in a mirror darkly. The elementary proof of this judgment is provided by the synthetic geometry known to Plato. The rediscovery of the root principle of synthetic geometry by Cusa, the isoperimetric principle, led to the solution for the problem posed by Plato, most notably the work of Gauss and Riemann.

The case of the Five Platonic Solids adduces the principled limitations of visible (e.g., Euclidean) space. There are certain forms, which exist as images in visible space, but yet which cannot be derived by construction from circular action. All of these forms have embedded in their construction some function of a complex variable (i.e., transcendental functions): functions derived from the elementary self-similar conical spiral. Moreover, circular action and its derivatives by synthetic-geometric construction are also determined as projections by functions of construction premised upon self-similar conic functions. This indicates that images in visible space, which cannot be entirely accounted for within the bounding geometrical characteristics of visible space, are fully accounted for as projected images of a higher-order space, the space of self-similar conical-spiral action.

Like Riemann,[6] we identify visible space as the *discrete manifold* and the higher space of self-similar conical-spiral constructions as the *continuous manifold*. We require that mathematics for physics be constructed entirely within the continuous manifold, and functions of the discrete manifold be accounted for mathematically as projections of images of the continuous manifold upon the visible (discrete) manifold. To this purpose, we require that the student employ the self-similar conical-spiral action to elaborate a synthetic geometry of continuous-manifold space in the same sense that circular action is employed to construct a synthetic geometry of visible space (the discrete manifold). All mathematics for physics

Karl Gauss

must be derived and proven mathematically solely by the synthetic-geometric method of construction within a continuous manifold, and algebraic functions treated as nothing more than descriptions of synthetic-geometric functions of a continuous manifold.

For us, as for Riemann,[7] experimental physics centers upon those *unique experiments* which prove mathematical (geometrical) hypotheses pertaining to the continuous manifold by means of experimental observations made in terms of the projected images of the discrete manifold. This possibility depends upon a geometrical principle of topology, *invariance*. In first approximation, *invariance* identifies those characteristic features of the geometry of a continuous manifold which are "preserved" through the process of projection as characteristics of the images of the discrete manifold. In

Bernhard Riemann   *Georg Cantor*

second approximation, higher-order invariances identify those changes in the continuous manifold which are carried over into the discrete manifold as transformations in invariants of the discrete manifold. *Relativistic transformations* in *the metrical properties of action* in the discrete manifold belong to this second, higher-order class of projective invariances. A *unique experiment* has as its subject-matter such a higher-order transformation in metrical characteristics of principles of action in a discrete manifold. Riemann's 1859 treatise on shock-wave generation is a model of the principles of *unique experiment*.

This principle of unique experiment is the key to the secret of the "curious phenomenon" which we broadly identified earlier.

The standpoint of Gauss, Riemann, et al., has several leading explicit features and implications which may appear profound to many readers of this text, but which we must at least identify here. These points identified bear significantly upon the topics to be encountered in following parts of the text.

First, the standpoint in physics of Riemann and the present writer is sometimes labeled the standpoint of the "ontological transfinite." This signifies, essentially, that the definition of "matter," "substance," ought not to be attributed to images in the discrete manifold, but only to the "real objects" of the continuous manifold. The "properties" attributed to "matter" must never differ from the definition of "matter" exclusively consistent with the mathematical physics of the continuous manifold as such. It is not that sense-objects do not correspond to something real, but that the way our minds perceive discreteness of objects in the visible (discrete) manifold is a distorted perception. In each case, we must find the reality within the continuous manifold which corresponds to the physical experiences perceived in terms of the discrete manifold.

The term "transfinite," used in that way, corresponds to the usage of Georg Cantor's (1845–1918) 1871–1883 publications on "transfinite orderings," expecially his 1883 *Grundlagen (Foundations of a General Theory of Manifolds)*. The foundations of this work of Cantor's were Riemannian approaches to trigonometric series and the related work of Cantor's teacher Karl Weierstrass (1815–1897), whose approach shaped Cantor's approach to Fourier analysis. "Transfinite," in Cantor's sense, flows from and implies a rigorously geometrical approach consistent with Riemann's.[8] Hence, the usage, "ontological transfinite," is not an inappropriate one.

The term "ontological transfinite" arose chiefly because of significant differences in method between Gauss and Riemann, on the one side, and the Göttingen of Professor Felix Klein (1849–1925), et al. Although Klein emphasized that the methods of discovery employed by Karl Gauss were being lost to modern knowledge, and mobilized efforts to revive this vanishing knowledge, the flaws in the work of the

great David Hilbert (1862–1943) show the loss of comprehension of principles of geometry employed by Gauss, Dirichlet, Riemann, et al., just as the great work of Max Planck
(1858–1947) on implications of black-body radiation, fails
by overthrowing mid-stream, in the elaboration of the quantum conception, the rigorous geometrical approach, in favor
of adapting to the doctrines of Clausius, Helmholtz, Boltzmann, et al. At best, the leaders in mathematical physics of
the European continent of the post-1860s generations defended the work of Kepler, Leibniz, Euler, Gauss, Riemann,
et al. against the empiricists' attacks, and defended the notion
of the "transfinite" as a mathematical conception. However,
they did not accept the proof that substantiality lies primitively
in the continuous manifold in the sense we have identified
the "ontological transfinite" here; hence, the later generations
indicated were associated with the "methodological transfinite," and so the distinction indicated was established.

A second point in the list provided here is the issue
reflected in the venomous campaigns against both Weierstrass
and Cantor by Leopold Kronecker (1823–1891). Kronecker,
who is responsible for some bad mathematics, promulgated
the maxim that "God created the integers," insisting that other
numbers were intellectual constructions. Pascal's elaboration
of the geometrical determination of differential number series,
Fermat's, Euler's, Dirichlet's, and Riemann's work on the
determination of prime numbers, illustrate the point that *all
numbers are generated by geometrical processes, and that this
determination belongs, in its entirety of scope, to the continuous manifold* (complex domain). Although students of Dirichlet at one point, both Kronecker and his friendly
competitor, Richard Dedekind (1831–1916), played a "hard
cop-soft cop" role in the center of a widespread conspiracy
to destroy Georg Cantor.[9] Kronecker's mathematics was a
blend of philosophical Cartesianism and British seventeenth-
century cabalism: like Descartes (1596–1650), Kronecker's
universe was limited to countable objects in Euclidean space,

a particular view feeding into the direction of such nominalistic radical extremes as the *Principia Mathematica* of Bertrand Russell (1872–1970) and A. N. Whitehead (1861–1947).

From survey of unpublished primary sources in archives, as well as published primary sources, the attack upon Cantor came from three cooperating directions. From France, it was the heritage of the operations of Laplace and Cauchy against the leading figures of the École Polytechnique (Fourier, Legendre, et al.). There was an element of religious persecution—outright inquisition against Cantor's mathematics—by elements of religious orders, which prompted Cantor at one point to appeal to the Pope against this. The third assault radiated from Britain, with Bertrand Russell for a time playing a leading part in this persecution. This continued a campaign explicitly directed against Gauss and Riemann from Britain, to which purpose James C. Maxwell's work was chiefly directed, according to Maxwell's own explicit declarations. Russell's illiterate invective against Riemann's 1854 habilitation dissertation is illustrative of the spirit in which Russell conducted his efforts to eradicate the reputations of Gauss, Riemann, Cantor and Felix Klein. Apart from the fact that Russell lived long enough to become the most evil single individual of the twentieth century, it is Russell who was at the center of the efforts to destroy Cantor's notion of the "transfinite," and to promote the fraud that modern "set theory" is the outgrowth of Cantor's work.

This astonishing conspiracy against Cantor is indicated to illustrate the force and magnitude of nineteenth-century efforts to eradicate the methodological (geometrical) heritage of Cusa, da Vinci, Kepler, Leibniz, Euler, Monge, Gauss, Riemann et al. The principal axiomatic and related defects spoiling present-day scientific work are chiefly products of the nineteenth-century inquisition typified by the case of Cantor. Similarly, conceptions proven valid beyond competent dispute, from work over the centuries from Cusa into the middle 1850s, now appear often eccentric mistakes among contemporary specialists who lack education in the history of the vicious brawls spilling over from the aftermath of the 1815 Congress of Vienna. Fortunately, through the efforts of hundreds of researchers combing through archive materials of a dozen nations over more than a decade, a large chunk of the truth of the internal history of modern science has been brought back into the light. Much of this has proven to have direct bearing on the principal issues internal to economic science. And, how could it be otherwise, since the central subject-matter of economic science is *technology?*

To summarize the immediately foregoing review of the special features of mathematical physics bearing directly upon economic science.

1) The real universe as a whole is negentropic, as is shown by critical scrutiny of Kepler's laws of astronomy, as by Gauss.

2) The real universe lies ontologically in the continuous manifold, a manifold mathematically explored by a synthetic geometry based on self-similar conical-spiral action. The visible world is a distorted projected image of the real world.

3) The kind of number which corresponds immediately to the reality of the physical world is of the form of complex numbers, complex numbers generated by synthetic-geometric constructions in the continuous manifold, the complex domain. The counting numbers are the projections of complex numbers into the visible world.

4) Knowledge of the physical world is derived from what Riemann defines as *unique experiments.*

Hence, the so-called Laws of Thermodynamics are false to physical reality, and are arbitrary postulates superimposed from the exterior upon scientific work. Most emphatically, any thermodynamics which requires these three putative Laws is entropic, a condition contrary to the proven fundamental ordering of the universe. Also, "energy" and "work," properly defined, correspond to realities existing within the continuous manifold, corresponding to complex functions not reducible to simple scalar magnitudes. "Energy" and "work" are not "things"; they are processes.

NOTES

1. Boltzmann died of suicide at Duino. See below.

2. This assumption was central to Karl Marx's false reasoning (*Capital III*, "Internal Contradictions") that the "rate of profit must tend to fall" in a capitalist economy. Although Marx repeatedly qualified his arguments, that he was leaving the calculable functions of technological progress out of account in this procedure, he consistently constructed his calculations for the conditions of expansion through re-investment on crude linear equations, prefiguring modern systems analysis (see text, below). There are several additional major errors in Marx's argument on this general point, but the one identified is central.

3. Statements to this effect, concerning the impact of the work of LaRouche, et al., were volunteered by leading policy-shapers of the Club of Rome, including Dr. Alexander King.

4. This construction for proving the principles of well-tempered polyphony was first proposed by LaRouche during a seminar, Spring 1981. The constructions were completed by Dr. Jonathan Tennenbaum, Rolf Schauerhammer, et al., and presented to a conference in West Germany later that year. This led into new work on reformulating the ontological-mathematical assumptions of Special Relativity (*Executive Intelligence Review*, New York, January 1983), and a preliminary survey of a Gaussian approach to modern applications of conically defined elliptic functions (Tennenbaum, Spring 1984).

5. *Cf.* B. Riemann, habilitation dissertation (1854).

6. *Ibid.*

7. *Ibid.*

8. Cantor's work is not congruent with "set theory" as the "new mathematics" represents that today. See text below.

9. LaRouche was put on the track of uncovering Dedekind's part in this ugly business by rereading Dedekind's 1872 preface to his paper on "Continuity and Irrational Numbers." Dedekind's role is merely one facet of what in entirety is best described as a nasty covert intelligence operation.

CHAPTER 4

The Definition of Economic Value

Our adopted mathematical function shows that a society (economy) becomes entropic unless there is technological progress to the effect of increasing the potential relative population-density. Hence, for the society (economy) as a whole, *economic value* is restricted to that quality of activities within a society which increases the potential relative population-density through the mediation of technological progress. In other words, *economic value* properly defined measures *the negentropy of the economic process*.

Economic value, so defined, and *work* have the same meaning.

It is not the quantity of effort applied, nor even the quantity of effort of a specific quality (e.g., skill-level, Marx's misdefinition of labor power, etc.) which defines *work*, nor is *work* measured by the quantity of physical-goods output, the price of labor, the price of the goods sold, and so forth and so on. No *scalar* measure of work is competent; no conception which might be expressed in terms of linear functions could possibly be competent. *Work* is irreducibly a non-linear magnitude, expressed by an irreducible function of a complex variable.

We may appear to differ with Leibniz on this point. In outward appearances, that is true; in method of approach, no. Discussion affords clarity in this matter. Recall our earlier description of Leibniz's use of the term *work*.

For purposes of initial approximation, Leibniz assumed that a certain variety of physical goods produced was

65

useful, to the point that more of the same was urgently wanted by society. On that account, the level of output of such goods by an operative served as an acceptable standard of comparison. In such terms of reference, the economy of labor accomplished by aid of a heat-powered machine is negentropic. It is not the amount of output of physical goods which measures work; *work* is measured in such a study as *the economy of labor accomplished*. It is the *economy of labor* as such which is the "micro-economic" empirical correlative of economic value.

Up to that point, the writer's definition of economic value does not differ either with Leibniz's, or the leading American System economists, nor with a principle understood and more or less efficiently served by most production managers with either an engineering background or an acquired equivalent sense of the production process. Every competent production manager the writer knew from his experience in management consulting and other encounters, agreed with the policy of practice of upgrading the workforce employed, while advancing technology along a capital-intensity pathway of investments. If contrary policies predominate in corporations with a competent production-management cadre, such contrary policies emanate from "Wall Street" financial interests and "Harvard Business school" types.[1]

The difference between Leibniz's treatment of the term *work* and the formulations of this text is merely one of refinement. The work of Gauss, Riemann, et al., as referenced in the preceding section, made possible a deeper insight into the principles of technology than Leibniz himself apparently supplied.[2] We may assume that Leibniz would endorse our refinement as fully consistent with his own direction of thinking on the matter. We are able today, to explore the deeper meaning of the term *work* to a degree not feasible under the conditions of development of science existing in Leibniz's time.

Before we elaborate some of the leading implications

of this non-linear definition of *economic value* in the terms of reference of the hypothetical, consolidated agro-industrial enterprise, it is time to identify some aspects of the importance of introducing and applying this "more sophisticated" conception.

By successive degrees of approximation thus far, we have repeatedly stressed the unity of technology, as the central fact of economic science, and technology from the standpoint of the fundamentals of mathematical physics, a unity underscored in the practice of leading circles of the École Polytechnique over the interval 1794–1815. If we desire to secure the optimal rate of advance of the economy of labor, we must define this not merely as a matter of investment policies, but a matter of what technologies are available for investment purchases. So, informed investment policies must become a science-investment policy, a policy governing allotments to investment in science as such. It happens to be the case, as will become increasingly clear in the remainder of this text, that the principles of technology, as we identify them here, bear directly upon the most fundamental features of scientific research. Consequently, the most intelligent investment policies center around not merely policies of investment in science, but policies of investments which promote specific areas of discovery bearing upon fundamental questions of mathematical physics, for example, accessible to inquiry during the immediate decades ahead.

On that account, a rigorous definition of economic value is required. To integrate the making of long-range decisions on investment in science with "return on investment" decisions in the production of physical goods, we require a measure of economic value equally applicable to scientific research and to the production process as such. That measure must address the fundamental principles of mathematical physics, for example, and measure at the same time and in the same way the fundamental determinants of economy of labor in the production process.

To provide a very practical demonstration of the point just made: Among so-called developing nations today, the best version of prevailing policies recommended to such nations by OECD nations, etc., is that the developing nations ought to adopt policies for "gradually overtaking" the levels of technology already established in leading OECD nations, for example. This implies that, at best, developing nations should ease slowly away from a colonial policy[3] of being predominantly raw-materials exporters, by opening their customs gateways to rations of hand-me-down industrial technology, with emphasis upon "import substitutions" in categories of consumer-goods production. The results of such policies have been wretched, especially for the developing nations. It is clear, for reasons to be defined in this text, that the leading edge of a development policy must be a commitment to leapfrogging some of the most advanced technologies currently in use in the United States, Europe, and Japan.

This requires the developing nation to select areas of scientific research in which it commits itself to become a world leader, as a matter of medium-term and long-range national commitment. It must parallel the development of laboratories, university departments, and scientific cadres to such ends, with a development of an industrial base for assimilating the products of scientific work. This latter must include emphasis on developing a relevant sort of tool-making industrial sector. The development of the science base and of the tool-making and other industrial-base elements must efficiently converge to the point of dovetailing within a generation or less.

The allotment of scarce national resources to this growing germ of future technological excellence must be balanced against and integrated with a more commonplace, but nonetheless urgent development of rural production, and so forth. For political reasons, and other practical reasons, the combined effort must show credible progress to the population generally, to most strata of the population as well as the majority of the population as a whole.

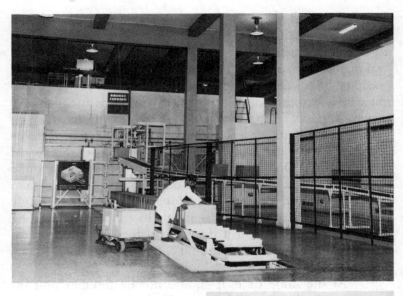

The underdeveloped nations must "leapfrog" the scientific and technological level of the industrialized sector. Above: nuclear energy is used to sterilize medical products at India's Babha Atomic Research Center in Trombay. At right: United Nations-sponsored "appropriate technology" in Kenya.

It should not be difficult to imagine the case of some anarcho-syndicalist demagogue howling imprecations against a government and business community which are allegedly "taking bread from the mouths of children" with investments in capital-goods development, or something akin to that. There must be a strong and well-informed consensus for medium- to long-term developmental policies in developing nations. To maintain that consensus, there must be a recognizable correlation between projected and achieved progress toward adopted goals. On that account, it is desirable that economic policy-making in developing nations be more rigorous than might be required for a more developed economy: the latitude to endure serious mistakes is much less in the developing nations. The mistake of a degree which to us might mean postponement of a few additional comforts, would be a margin of suffering in most developing nations.

At the same time, it should not be thought that investment in technological leapfrogging by a developing nation is a luxury for such nations, a discardable option. Without such leapfrogging, those nations would never cease to be underdeveloped. It is an unavoidable course of action, but not an easy course to manage.

In both extremes, the most advanced and the poorer developing nations, what is needed today is economic policies attuned to "science-driver" practices of rapid increase in the economy of labor. For this an improved policy-making instrument is required, a policy-making instrument which provides a common language for the scientists engaged in fundamental research and economic management.

This should be seen in the context of the three categories of fundamental research in which all fundamental technological progress of the coming fifty years or so will occur (assuming we cease our drift into the "new dark age" of "post-industrial society"). The fundamental scientific propositions posed in the three areas converge, not an unusual arrangement in the history of science; the terms of reference upon which they converge are the same terms we have identified in this text.

These three categories of fundamental research are: 1) Organized plasmas of very high energy-flux density, typified by progress in development of controlled thermonuclear fusion as a primary energy source for mankind; 2) The related area, development of high-energy-flux-dense coherent radiation as a tool of production and other applications, typified by development of lasers and particle beams; 3) New directions of fundamental breakthrough in biology, for which the important developments in progress in the field of microbiotechnology is but a very important auxiliary feature.[4] In a reasonable scheme of things, significant breakthroughs in all three areas should be a "commercial" fact of life by about the turn of the century. Combined, these three mean the feasibility of powered, manned interplanetary flight by near the turn of the century, and increasing practicability of colonies in Earth-simulated environments on the Moon and Mars not long afterwards.

These areas of fundamental breakthroughs, compared with one of their exemplary, combined applications, all require a shift to emphasis in research and applications to Riemannian physics, to the standpoint of the "ontological transfinite." We require a society which thinks and manages the development of its economy in those same principled terms of reference. We require economists within each and all of the professions who radiate this essential knowledge among their peers and into the society at large.

The analysis of the social division of labor in society (economy), as developed by Henry C. Carey and others,[5] impels us to the following accounting procedures for analysis of the internal relations of production and consumption of our hypothetical, consolidated agro-industrial enterprise. To this end, we employ some of the same symbology made fa-

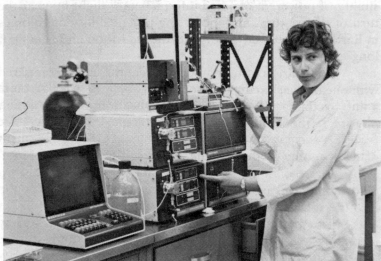

Above: Experiment in laser fusion at Lawrence Livermore Laboratories in California; directed energy beams are used to trigger the nuclear reaction. Below: A facility at Alfacell, Biotechnology can curb disease, increase food production, and transform industrial and metallurgical processes.

miliar by the Marxists and others; definitions of these symbols other than definitions of this text should be ignored as irrelevant.

Since we are measuring increase of potential relative population-density, we must begin with population. Since the unit of reproduction of the population is the household, we measure population first as a census of households, and count persons as members of households. We then define the labor force in terms of households, as labor-force members of households, as the labor force "produced" by households.

We define the labor force by means of analysis of the demographic composition of households. We analyze the population of the household first by age interval, and secondly by economic function.

Broadly, we assort the household population among three primary age groupings: 1) Below modal age for entry into the labor force, 2) Modal age range of the labor force, and 3) Above modal age range of the labor force. We subdivide the first among *infants, children under six years of age, pre-adolescents, and adolescents.* We subdivide the second primary age grouping approximately in decade-long age ranges. We subdivde the third primary age grouping by five-year age ranges (preferably, for actuarial reasons). We divide the second primary group into two functional categories: household and labor-force, obtaining an estimate such as "65% of the labor-force age range are members of the labor force."

We assort all households into two primary categories of function, according to the primary labor force function of that household. The fact that two members of the same household may fall into different functional categories of labor-force employment, or that a person may shift from one to the other functional category is irrelevant, since it is *change in the relative magnitudes* of the two functional categories which is more significant for us than the small margin of statistical error incurred by choosing one good, consistent accounting procedure for ambiguous instances. This primary functional assortment of households is between the *operatives* and *overhead-expense* categories of modal employment of associated labor-force members of those households.

At this point our emphasis shifts to the operatives' component of the total labor force. All calculations performed are based on 100% of this segment of the total labor force. The operatives' segment is divided between agricultural production, as broadly defined (fishing, forestry, etc.), and industrial production broadly defined (manufacturing, construction, mining, transportation, energy production and distribution, communications, and operatives otherwise employed in maintenance of basic economic infrastructure).

The analysis of production proceeds principally as defined earlier in the text. The analysis begins with the distinction between the two market-baskets and the two subcategories of each's final commodities. The flow of production is traced backwards through intermediate products and raw materials to natural resources.

This analysis of production flows is cross-compared with the following analysis of production of physical-goods output as a whole: 100% of the operatives' component of the labor force is compared with 100% of the physical-goods output of the society (economy). This 100% of physical-goods output is analyzed as follows.

Symbol V: The portion of total physical-goods output required by households of 100% of the operatives' segment. *Energy of the System.*

Symbol C: Capital goods consumed by production of physical goods, including costs of basic economic infrastructure of physical-goods production. This includes plant and machinery, maintenance of basic economic infrastructure, and a materials-in-progress inventory at the level required to maintain utilization of capacity. This includes only that portion of capital-goods output required as *Energy of the System.*

Symbol S: *Gross Operating Profit* (of the consolidated agro-industrial enterprise).

T [= total physical-goods output] $- (C + V) = S.$

Symbol D: *Total Overhead Expense.* This includes consumer goods (of households associated with overhead expense categories of employment of the labor force), plus capital-goods consumed by categories of overhead expense. *Energy of the System.*

Symbol S′: *Net Operating Profit* margin of physical-goods output. $(S - D) = S'.$ *Free Energy.*

If we reduce Overhead Expense (D) to a properly constructed economic-functional chart of accounts, there are elements of Services which must tend to increase with either increase of levels of physical-goods output or increase of productive powers of labor. For example: a function subsuming the notions of both level of technology in practice and rate of advancement of such technology specifies a required minimal level of culture of the labor force, which, in turn, subsumes educational requirements. Scientific and technical services to production and to maintenance of the productive powers of labor of members of households, are instances of the varieties of the accounting budgeter's Semi-Variable Expenses which have a clear functional relationship in magnitude to the maintenance and increase of the productive powers of labor. Large portions of Overhead Expense as a whole have no attributable functional determination of this sort; in a "post-industrial society" drift, the majority of all Overhead Expense allotments should not have been tolerated at all, or should have been savagely reduced in relative amount. For this reason, we must employ the parameter $S'/(C + V)$, rather than $S'/(C + V + D)$, as the correlative of the ratio of free energy of the system.

For purposes of National Income Accounting, we employ:

Symbol S/(C + V): *Productivity* (As distinct from "productive powers of labor").

Symbol D/(C + V): *Expense Ratio.*

Symbol C/V: *Capital-Intensity.*

Symbol S'/(C + V): *Rate of Profit.*

These ratios require the conditions: 1) That the market-basket of consumer goods per capita, for households of the operatives' segment of the labor force, increases in relative magnitude and quality of content as capital-intensity (C/V) and productivity $(S/C + V)$ increase. 2) That the social cost of producing this market-basket declines secularly, despite the required increase in magnitude and quality of its content. 3) That Productivity $(S/C + V)$ increases more rapidly than the Expense Ratio $(D/C + V)$.

The Chart of Accounts for National Income Accounting assorts Overhead Expense among three principal functional classifications of accounts: *Economic, Institutional,* and *Waste.* The distinctions are broadly as follows.

Economic: Services and Administrative functions essential to either *the process of production and physical distribution* or *the maintenance and development of households at levels consistent with the level and required rate of advancement of technology.*

Institutional: Expenses of Government's non-economic activities, including military, police, and essential administrative functions, for example. Expense of business and other non-governmental institutions, including selling expenses (as distinct from physical distribution costs), which are not Economic, but which are required as categories of expenditure dedicated to maintaining the existence of functions of the institution.

Waste: Expenses incurred by unemployment, expense to society of criminal activities, and expense to society incurred by activities which ought to be classified as immoral, if not explicitly criminal, including all forms of usury.

Classifications of services under the heading of *Economic* include:

Scientific Research: The physical sciences, including biology, economic science, and mathematics itself. History. Exploration. *But not:* psychology, sociology, anthropology, and kindred "ologies" of so-called "social science" as they are practiced today. Generally, Wilhelm von Humboldt's (1767–1835) policies for education define the competent forms of science and education.

Scientific, Engineering, and Related Technical Services either directly to the process of output of physical goods, or indirectly to the development and maintenance of elements of basic economic infrastructure which form part of the indispensable physical environment of production and physical distribution of such goods.

Medical and Related services to maintenance of the population.

Education based on principles consistent with those of Humboldt.

Other forms of services, especially "labor-intensive, unskilled or 'semi-skilled' services," are marginal, *Institutional,* or even *Waste.*

Classifications of administration under the heading of *Economic* include:

Direct Supervision of the employment of operatives.

Supervision of the economic functions of processes employing the labor of the operatives' segment of the labor force.

Excluded from *Economic* are items including:

Selling Expenses other than physical distribution of goods. (*Institutional*).

Finance Administration (including financial charges as such). Except for charges and administration of Usury (including Ground-Rent, Commodity-Price Speculation, etc.), which are classified under *Waste, Finance Administration* is an *Institutional* Expense.

Although Government is broadly classified under *Institutional* Expense, those activities of government which are Economic (production, maintenance of basic economic infrastructure, etc.) are classified as *Economic—Government,* and are analyzed in the same manner as private *Economic* functions.

Broadly, Overhead Expense is analyzed by asking the questions, "*In what way* is this Expense incurred?" And "*Why* is this Expense incurred, both as to category of expenditure, and relative amount of expenditure?" The students should develop complete Charts of Accounts of Overhead Expense for both sample business firms and entire economies, according to the policy specifications supplied here. This students' work, and other elaboration of Charts of Accounts of National Income Accounting, should be assigned at the phase of studies corresponding to completing study of the matters covered through this point of the present text. The students' work done to that effect at this point of the program should be retained for revision made at the completion of the program indicated by this text as a whole.

In the case of the scientific discoverer, for example, the individual's direct contribution to increase of the economy of labor is simple and clear. From this beginning point of reference, we must trace the pathways through which scientific and related discoveries are transmitted into and through the economic process as such, to the effect that operatives participate in transmitting negentropy to the society (economy) as a whole. It is this transmission of negentropy by the activity of operatives which is the "substance" of economic value. The preceding outline of the principal features of construction of a National Income Accounting's Chart of Accounts permits us to trace the connections chiefly to be considered.

Near the close of his essay, "In Defence of Poetry," Percy B. Shelley not inaccurately associates upsurges in quality and use of poetry with periods of history during which great upsurges in the struggle for civil and religious liberty have occurred. This is certainly the case for the republican movements of classical Greece, beginning about 599 B.C. with the constitutional reforms of Solon at Athens. It is the case for the fifteenth-century Golden Renaissance, and the work of Dante Alighieri (1265–1321) and his successor Petrarch (1304–1374) which organized the movement erupting as the Golden Renaissance. It was the case during the late seventeenth-century's post–1653 developments in Mazarin's (1602–1661) and Colbert's (1619–1683) rebuilding of France, in the developments associated with the Great Elector of Prussia and others in Germany. It was the case throughout Europe into the 1815 Congress of Vienna, under the influence of the great transatlantic conspiracy headed by Benjamin Franklin during the interval 1766–1789. Shelley himself echoed that 1766–1789 political and scientific upsurge.

In such periods there is, as Shelley puts the point, an increase in the capacity of populations for "imparting and receiving profound and impassioned conceptions respecting man and nature." In relatively modern centuries, beginning with Dante's De Vulgari Eloquentia and Commedia, non-Latin languages of Europe were developed into the highly literate classical languages they became in Italy, France, and England, for example, during the course of the late fifteenth into the close of the sixteenth centuries. The development of language, as Humboldt emphasizes, is a limitation upon the power of thinking, such that persons limited to a poor local dialect are condemned thus to be intellectually inferior in potential powers of judgment. Embedded within such functional implications of the degree of development of languages in use, there is a crucial feature which bears directly, and most practically, upon the question of economic science immediately before us here. The two variable qualities of speech which bear most significantly upon the speaker's power to think are the degree of emphasis placed upon ideas associated with transitive verbs, as opposed to nominalist emphasis on ideas peculiar to nouns, and the rigorous use of the subjunctive.[6] These functions of language bear implicitly and more or less directly also upon the level of development of the creative-mental processes within the individual and society.

The transmission of negentropy through the labor of operatives is the transmission of ideas, in Plato's sense of *species*.[7] Not "ideas" understood as description or explanation: *ideas as controllers of the actions of persons, practical actions to change nature to mankind's advantage*. We have assigned the systematic discussion of scientific ideas' internal characteristics to the following section of the text. At this stage of the present section, we are "borrowing" credit from that future part of the text to identify as much of the matter as is indispensable for stating what follows immediately here.

It is the creation, assimilation, transmission, and realization of those scientific and related discoveries whose practice represents *potential economy of labor*, which is the negentropic feature of the *social process of production of physical goods*. It is that aspect of the process of production which permits us to locate the economic value of the productive labor of individuals, *the aspect of individual activity which is immediately universal in its effects*.

It is a corollary of this, that the value of the output of a society (economy) cannot be determined by adding up the net prices (e.g., "value added") of the individual exchanges within the economy. If this error is perpetrated, we are led into the fallacy, the paradox, of Marx's "Internal Contradictions," in *Capital* III. Review of that paradox again, this time in terms of reference of National Income Accounting, aids us in isolating the empirical feature of the productive process in which the function of technological progress is most narrowly located.

Express the mathematical function of the changing ratio of free energy to energy of the system by substituting $S'/(C + V)$ for the free-energy ratio. Then, according to the set of constraints we specified above, the "re-investment" of S' increases the per capita magnitude of output represented by $(C + V)$. If the percentile of the labor force employed as operatives remains constant, without technological progress, the increased energy of the system per capita $(C + V)$ reduces the ration of S' available for re-investment in the succeeding cycles. Thus, it might appear, as capital-intensity (C/V) increases, the rate of profit $S'/(C + V)$ must fall.

Assume the hypothetical case, that a modern economy at some point adopts the policy decision to halt the process of incorporating innovations into new designs of capital goods. For a time, the economy would continue to grow. This could occur because the replacement of older stocks of capital goods by newer stocks would represent advancement of technology of production (economy of labor). As the average level of technology of capital stocks employed approaches the technological level of the new stocks, the benefit of re-investment would begin to vanish, and the falling rate of profit would fall to the degree that the economic process became entropic.[8]

Examine this aspect of the processs more closely.

"Re-investment" in capital stocks involves two elements of the Chart of Accounts: Net Operating Profit (S') and the current energy-of-the-system cost of accumulated investment in capital stocks (C). So, total "re-investment" in capital stocks ought to be in the order of $(S' + C)$, for the case the number of operatives employed remained constant over successive cycles.

We have measured these two magnitudes in terms of

the level of technology (economy of labor) at which current physical-goods output was produced. However, what if the capital goods produced represent a higher level of technology (economy of labor) in their application than the level of technology employed to produce them? In here, this precise location, lies the secret of the paradox, and the substance of negentropy in the economic process. Let us assume, for example, that new capital stocks are 5% more efficient (represent a relative 5% economy of labor), by comparison with the capital stocks employed to produce them. Then, the portion of present output allotted to energy of the system of the production process is only 95% of the amount suggested by simple National Income Accounting projections. Thus, the free energy re-invested becomes $(S' + 0.05C)$, rather than S'. The greater the ratio C/V, the greater the relative increase in free energy accomplished.

Negentropy in the economic process takes the form of changes in behavior of operatives in the production of physical-goods output, most emphatically capital-goods output. Hence, a high ratio of capital-goods to consumer-goods output is the more healthful circumstance of an economy undergoing technological progress. A highly skilled labor force of operatives, able to assimilate and employ those changes in behavior flowing from scientific discovery, is the optimal labor-force policy, and related general educational policy. The purpose of education for employment, as distinct from its other indispensable functions,[9] is as Humboldt required: rather than preparing pupils through secondary school for some specialized trade skill, *education must bring forth in the fullest possible degree the broadest potentialities of the child and youth, prior to specialist education to begin after the completion of secondary-school education.* The point is not to teach youth to behave in a fixed mode prescribed for them by standards of normal behavior developed up to the present time. The point is to develop the creative-mental potentialities of youth in the broadest possible scope, to supply them with rigorous methods for efficiently innovating (e.g., productive) behavior, assimilating those innovations into the form of fruitful transformations in day-to-day behavior (e.g., behavior in production).

The introduction of the heat-powered machine, or analogous capital-intensive changes in the technology of production, must be comprehended as an indispensable feature of a change in human behavior, *a change in mankind's practical relationship to nature as a whole.* The economy of labor, accomplished by this means, is a reflection of the fact that the scientific discovery generating such changes in behavior, embodies an increasing correspondence between the behavior of mankind and the lawful ordering of our universe. *The economy of labor in the productive process must be comprehended as the greatest of all scientific experiments:* the experiment which proves empirically, as nothing else can, those *principles of scientific discovery* upon which the authority of all scientific knowledge entirely depends.

No separation between fundamental scientific research and "applied science" will be tolerated by the people of a sensible nation. The object of fundamental scientific discovery is the changes in nature accomplished through the physical-goods output of the workshop, the changes in man's relationship to nature so accomplished. Physical Economy, economic science, is the principle of fundamental scientific discovery comprehended in these terms of reference; the scope of economic science, properly defined, extends from the final measure of scientific knowledge, at the end of the production line, backwards to the fundamental scientific discoveries upon whose continued proliferation the continuation of the process of production depends.

In that connection lies the location of the ultimate secret of economic value's determination: the principles of fundamental scientific discovery.

NOTES

1. During the second half of the 1950s, during the same general deliberations leading to adoption of Nuclear Deterrence, Flexible Response and Arms Control, leading circles in the "liberal Establishments" of London and the northeastern U.S.A. decided to push the world's economy into the direction of a "post-industrial" phase. "Back-channel" agreements with the Soviet government, reached through Bertrand Russell's and other channels during that period, persuaded these "liberal Establishments" that Nuclear Deterrence either precluded general warfare between the superpower alliances, or that if such a war began, it would cease at the point of completion of the opening barrages of "strategic" thermonuclear bombardments. Only "local wars," including perhaps "limited nuclear wars," each conducted within the guidelines of a flexible set of rules (Flexible Response), would be expected. Nuclear Deterrence was viewed, thus, as putting a cap on the military requirement for the in-depth logistical strength of a technologically progressive economy. The "post-industrial society" policy was advertised widely from the turn of the 1960s, and began to be put into operation as U.S. governmental policy during the middle 1960s, as typified by the coincidence between President Johnson's "Great Society" doctrine and the initial tearing down of the research-and-development commitments centered then around NASA.

   Since the "liberal Establishment" elements adopting this perspective were spokesmen for circles of European and North American family interests, virtually Italian-style *fondi* which control the dominant banking and insurance complexes, the flow of credit and investment funds into, and out of, corporations began to reflect increasingly the "post-industrial" orientation of the mid–1960s "head of the Establishment" (according to John K. Galbraith), McGeorge Bundy (at the Ford Foundation). Zbigniew Brzezinski's "technetronic society" thesis is a reflection of this indicated connection between "utopian" strategic thinking and social-economic policy thinking. The tendency grew, as illustrated by the case of U.S. Steel, to use industrial corporations as money-generators for investments in non-industrial ventures,

amounting to a policy of cannibalizing such firms being run into
the ground through disinvestment in the production process.

The pressures for such policies of industrial corporations
came not only in the form of direct pressures from Wall Street,
including the corporate raiders lurking to asset-strip any cor-
poration unable to defend its stock from such lurking wolves.
It also came from changes in thinking from the inside of managements. The role of the "Harvard Business School type" within
management, beginning with such types as Robert S. McNamara
at Ford and the Pentagon, is at the center of this change in the
philosophical outlook of industrial managements. This is aptly
reflected by comparing the readership-sensitive *Wall Street Journal*'s issues from the 1950s and early 1960s with the neo-liberal
mixed with neo-conservative philosophical outlook in recent
editions.

Harvard Business School is merely a prototype of what now
permeates graduate business schools world-wide. What is taught
in such locations is predominantly an ideology. What passes for
economic sophistication in such centers is merely old William
Petty's seventeenth-century doctrine of *buying cheap and selling
dear* mystified by a thick overlay of the late John von Neumann's
doctrine of "mathematical economics." The magic phrase is
"opportunity cost."

Although von Neumann was familiar with some of the algebraic description of Riemann's work, for example, his philosophical outlook was essentially that of Kronecker and
Dedekind, or of Laplace, Clausius, Helmholtz, Boltzmann. This
showed itself at its worst after Kurt Gödel's devastating attack
on certain of von Neumann's leading assumptions, about 1932
(e.g., *Gödel's Proof,* which should be read from the standpoint
of Cantor's 1871–1883 work). That worst was von Neumann's
application of his theory of games to economic processes. His
efforts to reduce economic analysis to solutions to systems of
linear inequalities, and his adoption of the radical ontological
assumptions of Viennese neo-positivist marginal utility, are exemplary of the reasons every system of econometric forecasting
based upon von Neumann's assumptions has failed so miserably.

Von Neumann's specifications for mathematical economics
require the assumption both that the economy is in a state of

zero technological growth, and that changes downward in the level of technology may be ignored. This approach, which saturates all known computer-based economic forecasting practice excepting the LaRouche-Riemann forecasts today, is the approach most consistent with the "post-industrial" policy direction noted.

The virtual brainwashing of business-school graduates and other professionals in a dogma so situated, and the concurrence of dominant forces of Wall Street, London, Switzerland, and Venice's insurance complexes, has infected much of U.S. industrial management with a change in philosophy of management so sharp it must be fairly described as a "cultural paradigm-shift."

2. "Apparently" is supplied here out of awe for what has been unearthed from amid the unpublished Leibniz archive, as well as fresh examinations of parts of Leibniz's published work in light of archives materials. Cusa's writings, those of Leonardo da Vinci, and also the writings of Kepler and Gauss, are of this same awesome quality. One must be most cautious in presuming from what one has studied of Leibniz thus far that he did not have something more than a prescience of fundamental discoveries attributed to someone at a later time.

3. Adam Smith's explicit policy from his *Wealth of Nations* is referenced here. It was against the British economic policies which Smith defended in that book that the American Revolution was fought.

4. As Pacioli and Leonardo da Vinci appear first to have shown, living processes are distinguished from non-living by a morphology of growth and developed functions consistent with the Golden Section. In other words, they are characteristically negentropic, as we have supplied the proper, synthetic-geometrical, Gaussian, definition of negentropy—rejecting the incompetent Wiener-Shannon "information theory" dogma. This signifies that organic chemistry per se is not a proper tool for determining the characteristic features of living processes; chemistry so narrowly considered has value for biology, of course, as the lessons of the dissecting table and pathologist's laboratories provide information useful to physicians concerned with maintaining the

healthy tissue of *living* persons. The elementary phenomenon of life must be geometrically congruent with the Golden Section, in terms of the discrete manifold, and must be of the form of negentropy as we have defined it here, in respect to the continuous manifold. If biology were to make this the *single empirical fact* upon which biology as a whole were reconstructed, the significance of chemistry would then be put into its proper perspective.

5. *Principles of Political Economy,* Vol. I, 1837, pp. 311–320, for Carey's extended quotation from Senior; Vol. II (1840), *passim* (on population), with special attention to Chapter IX. It is of interest to compare this three-volume work of Carey's and the other writings of Carey's known to Karl Marx, to see how bitterly Marx envied and hated Carey.

6. The putatively literate use of the English language had already fallen way below the quality of literate English during Shakespeare's and Milton's time during the 1950s, before the destructive impacts of Chomskyan linguistics and the argot of the rock-drug counterculture. The principal among the defects to be noted include the disuse of the subjunctive, and philosophical nominalism in manner of emphasis upon the noun as the natural unit of ideas. The first is the outgrowth of a steady campaign to eradicate the use of the subjunctive, by academics who recognized quite accurately the practical philosophical significance of the subjunctive as the medium for thinking in terms of scientific hypothesis. The emphasis upon the noun was also the fruit of campaigns on behalf of philosophical empiricism.

7. Criton Zoakos has pointed out that the word "Idea" is an improper and misleading translation; the best approximation in English is *species*. From the construction of Plato's arguments, there can be no reasonable doubt of the accuracy of Zoakos's proposed correction. The significance of this will become clearer in the following section of the text.

8. The U.S. economy entered a *relatively* entropic phase over the period 1966–1974. The U.S. economy became absolutely entropic—absolutely "negative economic growth rates," and operating below economic "breakeven"—within a few months after the policies jointly adopted by the Carter-Mondale Administra-

tion and Federal Reserve Chairman Paul Volcker during October 1979 went into effect.

9. *The function of citizenship* is the most general purpose of primary and secondary education. If members of the electorate cannot think, but can vote, what kind of elected government might we expect? Without rigorous training in rational thinking about any kind of topic on which a citizen might have to vote in choosing among candidates, what value does "public opinion" have bearing upon *truth* or determination of either national interests or the citizen's own immediate interests?

CHAPTER 5

How Technology Is Produced

The fundamental principles of fundamental scientific—and technological—breakthroughs are the same today as they were when Plato elaborated them more than 2,300 years ago. The matter permeates Plato's dialogues as a whole, in his repeated references to the subject of *hypothesis*. Without hypothesis nothing truthful and fundamental respecting man's relationship to the universe could be discovered. This was the method of Cusa,[1] Leonardo da Vinci,[2] Kepler, Leibniz, Gauss, Riemann, et al. In our intensive survey of the internal history of modern science's development, hundreds of researchers, working for approximately a decade or longer among various archives of the world and among primary published sources, have not discovered a case in which any valid fundamental discovery was produced in any other way than by this method of hypothesis.[3]

The principle of mental life governing fundamental scientific discoveries is termed by Plato *the hypothesis of the higher hypothesis,* a conception which is at the center of Plato's entire work. Who does not know and employ this principle knows nothing essential of Plato's work, cannot "get inside his mind." We elaborate that principle here, in modern terms of reference. We proceed from that to show the connection between mental life organized according to this principle and the origin of economic value in social processes (economies).

The notion of a Hypothesis of the Higher Hypothesis defines three levels of formation of hypotheses. The first of these levels we identify as *Simple Hypothesis,* the second *Higher Hypothesis,* and the third *Hypothesis of the Higher Hypothesis.* We describe these now by comparing these forms of hypothesis with the kind of thinking associated with a logical-deductive, interconnected network of theorems, each and all based (conditional) upon an underlying set of axioms and postulates.

In the case of Simple Hypothesis, the doctrine of some existing body of knowledge or opinion is applied to some phenomenon chosen as the subject-matter of simple or experimental observation. In the experimental hypothesis, or "design of experiment," so formulated, nothing is permitted which contradicts the established axioms and postulates underlying the doctrine employed. Logical-deductive *consistency* of the experimental results with the entirety of the existing doctrine is the standard of proof.

In the case of Higher Hypothesis, the authority of some existing doctrine is overthrown. The subject of the simple or experimental observation is one or more of the axiomatic assumptions of a prevailing doctrine. An experimental case is selected such that if anticipated experimental results are obtained, the subject axiomatic features of existing doctrine are proven to be everywhere false. Such proof signifies that each and every theorem of existing doctrine dependent upon the "hereditary" implications of that axiomatic feature of the doctrine must be discarded, and the latticework of that entire doctrine reconstructed on the basis of the newly proven principle. *Such is the nature of fundamental scientific discoveries.* All fundamental scientific discoveries are accomplished by employing that state of mental processes defined by Higher Hypothesis.

The historical fact of human progress, interpreted with aid of the internal history of progress of known science, shows that the succession of fundamental discoveries responsible for human progress is implicitly an orderable series. Each fundamental discovery establishes a revised body of scientific knowledge; the successful elaboration of this knowledge for practice leads into paradoxes prompting a new fundamental discovery, and a revised body of scientific knowledge, overturning its predecessor. Therefore, the authority of science cannot be located within the confines of any present or past body of scientific opinion. The authority of science lies in those principles of fundamental discovery which are contained in *none* of the mutually contradictory features of successive generations of scientific opinion. *The authority of science lies in principles of discovery adequate to generate each and all of a series of successive, successful scientific revolutions.*

A valid Higher Hypothesis does not leap out of nowhere, as if by blind intuition. A Higher Hypothesis is produced by a method, a method of formulating such discoveries. A simple or experimental observation which tests supposed criteria for formulating valid Higher Hypotheses, is an empirical inquiry into a set of principles corresponding to a *Hypothesis of the Higher Hypothesis.*

Although principles of discovery so empirically proven are universally valid, they are never perfected. *They remain a form of hypothesis in the sense that they are not perfected.* As science progresses through successive revolutions, the imperfection of the principles tends to lessen, without becoming yet perfected. These principles are the principles embedded in the conception of a synthetic-geometrical method of rigorous thinking. The isoperimetric principle is an example of discovery of an imperfected Hypothesis of the Higher Hypothesis. The work of Gauss, Dirichlet, Riemann, et al. on the synthetic geometry of a continuous manifold (complex domain) is an example of the process of perfecting the Hypothesis of the Higher Hypothesis. Riemann's 1854 habilitation dissertation, "On the Hypotheses Which Underlie Geometry," is a hypothesis governing the formation of higher hypotheses for synthetic geometry, and is therefore an explicit statement on the subject of perfecting the Hypothesis of the Higher Hypothesis. Indeed each of the writer's principal discoveries in economic science have been obtained chiefly by following the program of that habilitation dissertation, by understanding its significance in the sense stipulated here, through aid of previous saturation in Cantor's conception of transfinite orderings. *No willfully directed fundamental discovery can be accomplished except by consciously self-disciplining one's mental life according to this sense of a principle corresponding to an Hypothesis of the Higher Hypothesis.* Others, lacking that conscious sense of the matter, may indeed contribute very important discoveries bearing upon fundamentals. Those others may know to a large degree *how* their discovery was accomplished. Those others could never, in that state of mind, know *why* they made that discovery.

You wish to change one of the fundamental axioms of some generally accepted scientific doctrine? It annoys you, there is a noticeable smell of falsehood or superficiality in that axiomatic assumption? How shall you revolutionize science, therefore? Shall you strike out blindly, randomly at the suspicious assumption? Shall you be informed by "feeling," by "intuition"? Good luck, then; with such blind groping you will need much luck to hit upon the right approaches. Or, shall you subject that offending axiomatic assumption to "deep epistemological analysis": what state of mind would cause someone to introduce such an axiomatic assumption? What is contrary to the lawful ordering of the universe in that state of mind? What is the false assumption underlying the formulation of such an axiom? That hidden but necessary assumption is your intended victim's "Achilles Heel"! Strike him there, and if that assault is not fruitful, then try to strike him precisely here! You must proceed from a consciousness of the fundamental principles underlying the production of successful Higher Hypotheses. That is your road map to discovery.

This leads us directly to our next, interlocking point to be presented here. Some otherwise quite respectable and intelligent people are strongly attached to a superstitious, perhaps religious belief in the existence of an entity whose existence has never been required by any experimental evidence: the fabled *quark*. A considerable amount of energy of mathematicians and scientists is annually wasted on this nonexistent little fellow, the quark; it is even the subject of a Nobel Prize.[4] Why this obsession about creating new costuming to adorn a tiny little creature which, to put the point most gently, no one so far has proven actually to exist?

After reading some of the literature of the quark sect, one is astonished to find that some of the adherents are otherwise quite sensible fellows, some genuinely gifted, even brilliantly so. Their quark theology sounds mathematically quite sensible, or to put the point more precisely, very, very, logical. The quark is purely a creation of formal deduction, like the culprit in a Sherlock Holmes mystery fiction. The quark's existence and richly elaborated mathematical qualities are the mirror image of estimated dates for the alleged universal "Big Bang" in the cosmos. Neither the quark nor the "Big Bang" are products of experimental physics. They come into existence entirely as by-products of the axiomatic features embedded in the choice of mathematics employed. The quark and Big Bang exist merely as postulates of a syllogistic latticework; they are postulated assumptions, arbitrarily introduced, whose purpose is to fill up some gaping hole in the mathematical system in question. For example, if we employ a mathematics derived entirely from synthetic geometry, the imaginary quark and imaginary Big Bang are shown to be things which simply never happened.

The "Big Bang" dogma is very old. Its first elaboration in modern form was by Aristotle; the first available refutation of Aristotle's Big Bang is by Philo of Alexandria, who proved that Aristotle's argument requires the "God is dead" thesis of the sort resurrected by the Nazi prototype Friedrich Nietzsche. None of the putative evidence submitted by some astrophysicists recently contains an element of proof that was not exposed as incompetent 2,000 years ago. Whenever one employs a mathematics for physics which is consistent with Aristotle's principles, sooner or later one of the users of that mathematics will announce that he has *mathematical proof* of the existence of the Big Bang; the quark is a postulated, fictional existence of the same parentage as the Big Bang.

The reason the quark superstition has persisted as long as it has is that defenders of the little critter's existence demand that they be subjected to no argument against the quark's existence, except arguments couched in terms of the kind of mathematics employed to invent the little fellow. Naturally, as long as the discussion is limited to such mathematics, the members of the quark sect will be reinforced in their faith; if valid, conclusive proof is to be submitted, this must employ a choice of mathematics language which the true believers abhor to speak. The result is the same as if their entire mathematics had been constructed on the article of faith, that the quark exists; then, that mathematics is employed to prove that the quark does exist.

Unfortunately, some people who know a great deal about advanced mathematics know nothing about the axioms (hypotheses) upon which the construction of the entirety depends. The complementary point is to be made, that they have no efficient comprehension of what is sometimes called the "hereditary principle" of theorem latticeworks, that every theorem added to such a latticework is permeated with the axiomatic assumptions employed to begin construction of the latticework. If one swallows unquestioningly Descartes' terrible misrepresentation of the physical world, as little hard balls roaming about in empty, Euclidean space, and accepts also the axiomatic arithmetic assumptions of fellows such as Kronecker and Dedekind, one already believes implicitly in both the Big Bang and the quark, whether or not one ever references an astronomical observation or other physical experiment.

The clinical case of the quark has been cited to make

more sensuous the significance for science of the next point to which we are turning here.

The great Sanskrit philologist Panini[5] stipulated that all words are derived from verbs. The contrary, Aristotelean thesis, embedded in Latin grammar and its derivatives, insists that nouns as names for objects toward which one might point, are primary. Aristotelean nominalism is the subsuming characteristic of the principle of the syllogism: causal action is excluded from the Aristotelean system, where for causal action the principle of the middle term is substituted. The same result is the characteristic of the Cartesian system. *Properties* (e.g., attributes) of things (nouns) are assumed to determine interaction, rather than any causal principles of physical space as a whole. To understand both Higher Hypothesis and the Hypothesis of the Higher Hypothesis, it is indispensable to explore the essential difference between empirical facts as defined from the standpoint of transitive verbs and the different definition of fact subsumed by nominalism. Forgive us, but we must touch on elements of theology here, since it is in theology that mankind has traditionally located reflections on these scientific matters.

An empirical fact, as defined by reference to the notion of a transitive verb, defines as irreducible a specific transformation occurring during finite time in finite space. Axiomatic "points" do not exist, but only "points" as singularities defined by folding a circle twice against itself. Thus, *physical* has the meaning of *transformation* (as opposed to static, particular existence instantaneously). Transformation exists only in finite time and finite spatial displacement. Hence, neither matter, nor space, nor time can be separated as existing independently of the other two. Matter in itself, space by itself, and time in itself, are meaningless constructs of a deluded mind. Only *physical space-time* exists.

Empirical facts, as defined in terms of transitive verbs, have kinships to other facts through either sharing in common the same transitive verb, or through that verb's discoverable connection to other transitive verbs. Thus, for Plato, empirical facts equally corresponding to a particular choice of use of a transitive verb, constitute a *species*. This is the root principle of that feature of Platonic method to which the label "Platonic Ideas" is usually attached.

Transformation generally is of the species-form of "coming into existence." All transformations have this common quality. This requires a transitive verb for a universality of coming into existence, to correspond to the existence of the whole universe as a transformation in physical space-time. Since it is the universe, the verb must be self-reflexive: "That which elaborates its own continuing transformation," which, rather than the King James Authorized Version translation, is probably the original intent of Jehovah/Yaweh. This form of self-reflexive verb is of well-defined usage in existing languages, particularly those literate forms of language whose philosophical outlook is congruent with Panini's on the subject of the verb.

It is readily recognized that we have required, as does Plato, the existence of a universal, unhypothesized principle, toward which the perfection of the Hypothesis of the Higher Hypothesis is directed. The recognition of the self-evidence of circular action in visible space, by aid of the isoperimetric principle, and the corrected (more perfected) discovery of the synthetic geometry of the continuous manifold, as premised upon the self-evident existence of self-similar conical-spiral action, are approximations the self-reflexive verb form: "That which elaborates its own continuing transformation." The latter identifies by name *an unhypothesized universal principle;* the methods of synthetic geometry identify a perfectible but otherwise corresponding Hypothesis of the Higher Hypothesis.

Unlike the nominalists, for us causality exists, and is embodied within the empirical facts of scientific work, the transformation-species of physical space-time. Those transformation-species represent our empirical data; that physical space-time is for us *substantiality,* what is *ontologically* real. For us, the "thing" of the nominalists is simply a "topological singularity" of a transformation, a singularity of physical space-time. Science, for them, is stringing imaginary self-evident things, like beads on a string, on the latticework of a nominalist's deductive-theorem latticework, or, similarly, chopping small things into ever-smaller constituent things— such as imaginary quarks. Science, for us, is centrally occupied with creating singularities; among us, the work most admired is the creation of a new species of singularity in physical space-time, as the case of Riemann's 1859 treatise on the propagation of acoustical shock waves illustrates this point.

The prototype of production of a singularity is the fact, that in an implicitly finite iteration of elliptical cross-sections of intervals of self-similar conical-spiral action, the termination of that iterative series of ellipses defines a finite magnitude of displacement: a finite volume, a finite length. Physically, in the case of an approximately cylindrical form of self-similar conical-spiral action in physical space-time, this is equivalent to a shortest wave-length at which coherent electromagnetic radiation can be propagated, for example. For mathematical-physics reasons, particularly in respect to differential characteristics of electrodynamic action, such a singularity as this conjectured shortest wave-length must be the complementary expression of a finite speed of light. This signifies, if valid, that our universe must be topologically finite, as other evidence shows independently.[6] This means that any negentropic action acts against a finite number of conditions of the universe, so determining a finite iterative, elliptical subdivision of the negentropic action. We are led to exploring in such directions by the standpoint of the transitive verb. The universe created itself as a continuing process of negentropic self-transformation; hence, the elementary form of universal action must be the universe's work against itself, to such effect that it is the elaborated "complexity" of the universe's self-elaboration to date which must be uniquely the ultimately bounding condition acting upon each new negentropic action.

In attention to matters of fundamentals, science must shift away from narrow focus on particular evidence of scientific work, yet without losing sight of that particularity. The terms "fundamental" and "universal" are coherent terms. In universality, we seek species of transformations common to highly dissimilar classes of experience, which are provably characteristic of each and all. Such proven species of transformations are relatively the *fundamental* facts of science.

In life on Earth, we have available to us only two well-defined classes of particular experience which correspond in fundamental species-distinctions to the negentropic universe implicitly proven to exist by proof of Kepler's astronomical laws. These are living processes generally, and the negentropic behavior of entire societies (economies). In biology, we have made poor progress, chiefly for reasons of oversight and misdirection, toward mastering the principles of living processes as *living processes*. We have made better progress on this account in Physical Economy (economic science). Hence, instantly we prove a principle of negentropic transformation in the domain of economic science, we must rush to astronomy, glancing at biology generally as we pass; we must uncover in the universality of astronomy the species of transformation we have discovered within the bounds of inquiry of economic science. Thence, we must come to the laboratories, and discover which line of inquiry verges most closely, by its nature, on some important aspect of negentropic processes. What we search out is never something very complicated, at least not in the sense of the nominalists' complicated theorem latticeworks. What we seek will always be very elementary once we discover it.

It is not necessary always to conjecture the right answer in these matters. It were better to be slightly "wild," on the condition that rigorous principles of discovery containing that "wildness," are always present as its energetic conscience. Hit on all interesting fronts simultaneously, shake every interesting tree to discover what fruit it bears; cultivate a "wildly" omnivorous appetite for startling discoveries, as universal an appetite as education and experience can equip one to master. In that way, governed by such a rigorous conscience respecting what one regards as probable hypothesis or proven, seek species of transformations that are more universal, and therefore more fundamental.

Let us call the nominalists the "bead-stringers." From Aristotelean "bead-stringing" itself no new and valid discovery could be produced by such methods—at least no profound discovery. Yet, from time to time, a person trained and apparently habituated to such "bead-stringing" produces something of importance, a significant discovery. In some cases, such discovery erupts not infrequently. Often, when he might feel called upon to explain such discovery, an honest, reflective "bead-stringer" will report that indeed the discovery was not accomplished by accredited "bead-stringing" procedures; it came into the "bead-stringing" world of practice as if from the outside, from a source which does not exist, and is not permitted to exist within the domain of "bead-stringing." Perhaps he calls this outside source "intuition." He might report that it were prudent to balance one's life, to the effect that occasional intellectual vacations from "bead-stringing" were enjoyed, vacations in the form of seemingly wild excursions of the intellect. Most of the popularized interpretations of "intuition" as a source of scientific discovery were better passed by; there is no rigor in any of them examined thus far. What confronts us in the indicated sort of case is an unconscious assimilation of the principle of Higher Hypothesis, something "censored" out of consciousness by the need to obtain better than passing grades amid the drill and grill of indoctrination in a syllogistic mathematical physics (for example). The part of the mind which revolts against this conditioning process is caused to appear a shameful part of the student's self, an aspect of his "fantasy life" he must hide from authorities and peers if he is not to become the subject of ridicule in his profession. It is this aspect of the discoverer's mind which may be regarded, wrongly but understandably, as "intuition."

"Intuition," to the extent something properly incurring that epithet exists, is an infantile, irrational impulse, a relic of what Adam Smith described as "original and immediate instincts." It is contrary to the nature of such an infantile beast-relic embedded within us to occupy itself with producing Higher Hypotheses, to think universally or in a synthetic-geometric mode. What some scientific discoverers identify as the faculty of "intuition," is in fact a well-educated, if more or less unconscious aspect of their mental life. This education must tend to occur "silently," but rather efficiently, in the course of a student's life, to the extent that the student develops a sense of geometric construction of species of conceptions: perhaps, in the case of a student "on the track" to a career in physics, through help of teachers or others who insist that the student work through for himself the step-by-step proof of each idea assimilated. The student is thus assimilating the experience of rediscovery of what scientists have discovered before him. If a student experienced Jacob Steiner's curriculum for synthetic geometry, and acquired the habit of thinking in such a way, even unconsciously, he would thus assimilate, even unconsciously, the kind of educated unconscious capacity for rigorous insight sometimes attributed to "intuition."

The principle of discovery is experienced by most civilized persons to one degree or another. In the commonplace, it is akin to a memory "on the tip of my tongue." In the case of discovery of something new to one's knowledge, as opposed to struggling with the tricks memory sometimes plays, one abruptly hears oneself thinking something one has never thought before; abruptly, it is simply "there," and one has a strong emotional sense of its "rightness," in the same way one recognizes the rightness of the name or whatever one was struggling to bring beyond the "tip of my tongue." This emotional feeling of the "rightness" of the discovery does not mean that the discovery is valid, but only that it is a discovery. Ordinarily, the latent power of discovery in the person is unconscious. In our experience, it is as if it exists unseen behind a locked doorway to a room in one's mind. One passes notes under the door to the unseen creature in the room beyond; one waits, in hope that a message will be returned. We hear the creature bustling toward the other side of the door; we are alert; something is on the tip of our tongue; we are about to receive a message, we hope, from the fellow, or whatever it is, behind that door.

Sometimes, we educate the creature, whatever it is. Our conscious thoughts inform it; we conduct a curious sort of silent dialogue with it. If we are fortunate, we discover that the creature, whatever else it may be, has a natural talent for synthetic geometry. Whether unintentionally, or consciously, we may act in ways which have the effect of educating the creature by teasing it with geometry problems, or framing the information we transmit to it in geometric terms of reference. Meanwhile, it seems always to be listening at the doorway, overhearing everything we think. If we stay on reasonably amiable terms with the creature, and supply it the material it needs for its education, we will exhibit a relatively greater degree of creative intelligence to the exterior world.

If we master the Hypothesis of the Higher Hypothesis adequately, the door is unlocked, and the creature we confront we recognize as our self.

This imagery is supplied to the practical point of attempting to render as sensuous as possible to the reader a sense of a practical approach to fostering the creative powers of mind. In addition to the strong desirability of affording to all our children the species of education implicitly proposed by this text, we should attend to the matter of implicit education of each and all in our society, to educate implicitly the creature behind the locked door as well as might be managed.

To pin this point down, another point must be registered now.

We all must have noted how our concentration span is bounded in scope and duration. Certain topics and species of thinking are unpleasant to us: the mind refuses to concentrate upon them. Or, even respecting topics more agreeable to us, the concentration fades. If we reflect more carefully on such phenomena, we may recognize that our emotional life has much to do with the manner our concentration span is variously bounded. We might recognize the evidence, that the characteristic feature of this emotional process, the common species-characteristic of the different colors of emotion involved, is *a sense of personal identity*. When a matter elates us with either joy or anger, for example, the colors of the subject-matter become more vivid. In other connections, blind rage may shut off unwanted subject-matters. And, so forth and so on. As to duration of concentration span, it is similar, although somewhat different. In part it is the same; the subject-matters to which concentration upon an initial subject-matter lead us, prompt reactions of the same sort as the initial subject-matter. There is something else, something of special importance in respect to processes of discovery. In addition to reacting to the subsumed subject-matters of a period of concentration, we react also to the characteristic features of the process subsuming the ordering of these subject-matters. We react to such characteristics emotionally, as well. Again, it is *our sense of personal social identity* on which these emotions pivot.

For example, the idea of being a certain kind of scientific worker gives preference not only to certain subject-matters but to the pleasure of experiencing in one's mind the quality of elaborated concentration one associates with the identity of being such a scientific worker. In the case of the person who rejects such a social identity for himself or herself, as with the case of the young woman conditioned to believe that thinking verging upon the scientific is "unfeminine," makes her a "less attractive woman," to experience such thinking in the elaboration of one's concentration is aversive in itself; the mind shuts down the effort, and the concentration fades.

The implicit education of populations for high rates of technological progress requires the proliferation of a kind of sense of social identity consistent with creative-mental activity of somewhat extended concentration span. This is necessary for the problem-solving aspects of the assimilation and application of new discoveries, as well as their propagation. This is fostered by placing a greater social value on the persons who succeed in such efforts than those who avoid them. This should not be simply a matter of cultural paradigms of "other-directedness"; it should not be a matter of reducing a person's self-image to another's mere opinion of him. The objective must be to foster an "inner-directed" sense that the individual who contributes to society in this way is an important as well as useful individual because of not only his creative powers, but his commitment to further development and beneficial use of those powers. What is needed is not a mirror-image of the supposed opinion of one in the minds of others (authorities, peers, etc.), but an inner moral sense of identity.

This point is made clearer by noting highlights of the manner in which the prevailing culture of the United States has been destroyed during the recent two decades. Since the middle 1960s, most emphatically, there has been a cultural paradigm-shift in the official morality of "popular opinion" (as certified by major news media and entertainment media), away from the values of rationality, technological progress, and future-orientation, to the countercultural values of a "Now" and "Me" generation. In sum: a regression of the culture toward hedonistic irrationalism, radical existentialism. Rather than attempting the necessarily long discussion of this cultural paradigm-shift, we limit the discussion to

The United States has suffered a paradigm-shift away from the values of technological progress, toward hedonistic irrationalism. Above: a "gay liberation" contingent in New York City. Right: Building New York's Verrazano Bridge in the early 1960s.

summarizing some highlights, as will be sufficient to make the point.

The kernel of the manipulation of public opinion and morals was the interdependency of the "sexual liberation revolution," as typified by the drug-lobbying pornographic *Playboy* since the early 1950s, and the increasing relegation of the employment of operatives to a "lower-class" status image. "Playboy" was the right name for the countercultural movement as a whole. The principle was and remains: hedonistic irrationalism, a regression to an infantile intellectual and moral state of mind catalyzed by offering of escapist fantasy life into the domain of sexual and related orgies. This overlapped the

suburban movement of the fifties: a value-shift away from
urban industrial life within households predominantly rooted
in the population of operatives.

Exemplary of the value-shift is the ejaculation: "I'm a
vice-president for my company, and my plumber earns a higher
hourly wage than I do!" The "junior executive," an office
boy with college degrees, asked where to obtain an application
blank for the John Birch Society, or something of that sort,

upon hearing for the tenth time or so that union members at some factory were earning higher wages than such an important contributor to our nation's prosperity as himself. The general observation to be made is clear enough. Such insecure "white-collar" strata were the broad social base for the "Playboy" revolution. There was no justification in economic science for the kind of shift in composition of the labor force associated with this cultural value-shift. Concomitant with that, the "skills" of the burgeoning "white-collar class" were scarcely indispensable to the economy in the sense skilled industrial operatives are. Many of the new "white-collar class" dreamed they were on the upward climb toward the lower ranks of the rich, but most of them found the ascent like walking up a tightrope, and the fear of falling off was always lurking. Their status, as it was and as they imagined it to be, was a precarious one. Accompanying this was a philosophy to the effect "the secret of getting ahead in life is cheating." Cheat any day, in one way or another, including in the forms of the "sexual revolution." The most important thing was not that it happened, but the social values attached to its happening.

Sensuous reality was shifted from "what you build" to the "recreation" you can afford, and the recreation became an increasingly seamy sort of plunge into what had once been the forbidden delights. The children of suburbia and its mystique exploded during the middle to late 1960s, and the parents adapted to what they rapidly despaired of attempting to change. In 1969, Henry Kissinger entered symbolically and substantively into the position of National Security Advisor, and the "environmentalist" movements and population reduction programs introduced in pilot form under President Johnson were unleashed upon a young population demoralized by the image of a society enmired in an endless and purposeless war in Vietnam. The image of a United States with a global purpose for existing was shattered; Friedrich Nietzsche's proposed transformation of values made rapid and accelerating headway, and the outcome of the suburban mystique and "Playboy countercultural revolution" (of infantile, hedonistic irrationalism) was the transformation of the young and the liberals generally into a Jacobin-like horde delighting in nothing so much as tearing the economy down, piece by piece, all in the name of either neo-Malthusian anti-technology causes, or delight in the victory of irrationalist "sensibilities" of some "militant group" over the image of authority of technological progress.

The cultural paradigm-shift induced in much of the population of the United States was not without such precedents as the Jacobin Terror in France, or the vast Young Europe radical upsurge led by Giuseppe Mazzini during the middle of the nineteenth century.

No longer is the human mind's creative potentiality a source of value placed upon the individual by "public opinion." Those characteristic features of concentration span associated with the power to assimilate new discoveries are being turned off by the action of an irrationalist's choice of personal social identity. Without a reversal of this trend in public opinion, a cultural paradigm-shift to a moral, rational sense of identity within the setting of technological progress, the United States is soon doomed to be virtually extinct through the moral decay within it.

If we may assume that the urgently wanted cultural paradigm-shift occurs, the emphasis in employment patterns must be on three critical points:

1) Raising the percentile of employed operatives within the total labor force to about 50% of the labor force.
2) Concentrating the increase in expansion of the capital goods producing sector of industrial production.
3) Increasing employment in research and development to the range of 5% of the labor force.

This must be aided with corresponding shifts in tax burdens, credit policies, and wage-rate policies. It will require a reversal of recent trends in public education, toward Humboldt's program for classical education, and including mandatory education in synthetic geometry from a primary level (begun as constructive geometric play-education). In addition to the economic-practical need for such a shift, the cultural-paradigm shift, as this affects the sense of personal identity of the individual in society, must be consciously fostered.

In this setting, we require the development of seed-crystal laboratories-*cum*-training centers, which provide a rigorous training of gifted young scientific workers in mathematical physics from the standpoint of synthetic geometry. There must be an accompanying emphasis upon the internal history of science from the standpoint of primary sources. In this context, the principles of the Hypothesis of the Higher Hypothesis must be made conscious. This approach, modeled upon the successful "educational brigades" program of Monge at the École Polytechnique, should be directed to turning out "brigades" of researchers and teachers for laboratories, universities, and industrial research-and-development programs throughout the republic. These centers must foster not only the creative scientific potentials of their members and graduates. A sense of direction must be developed, respecting those frontiers of fundamental breakthrough which our science must master in the generation ahead.

Added to this, the proliferation of knowledge and use of a form of economic science which links directly the production of economic value and fundamental issues of scientific research, will provide the basis for coherence between economic management and research, which a "science-driver" national policy implies.

NOTES

1. On Cusa's scientific method generally, the preferred choice of a single source is Cusa's *De Docta Ignorantia* (*On Learned Ignorance*). For Cusa's own replication of Plato's Hypothesis of

the Higher Hypothesis, the most concentrated representation is Cusa's *De Non Aliud (On the The Non-Other).*

2. Perhaps the most useful single source for study of the breadth of Leonardo's work, was published in Italy in 1938, of which an excellent second edition in English translation is extant: *Leonardo da Vinci,* New York (undated, Italian copyright), 534 pp., folio, with excellent reproductions of paintings and sketches in a liberally illustrated edition. The book is the outgrowth of a pre-war symposium in Milan, and is a compilation of topical sections by various specialists. The specialists were mistaken in parts, sometimes on important or otherwise significant points, but Leonardo's own views and those of the commentators are for the most part conveniently distinguished. In a well-ordered educational program, every pupil would have worked through the scope of this book before graduating from secondary school. The point to be made, in this immediate portion of our text, is not only that Leonardo's enormous scientific fertility was derived from his mastery of Plato's and Cusa's *method,* but that he was emphatically, constantly conscious of the connection between his method and his discoveries.

Among his many significant discoveries, produced directly on the basis of this method, was his discovery that energy is radiated (e.g., light) at a definite speed of propagation, and that the radiation is in the form of transverse wave-motion. He insisted that all wave-motion was transverse, including sound waves. The latter was assumed to have been an error in later times, until Riemann's 1859 treatise on the propagation of acoustical shock waves. (Leonardo based most of his developments in energy-radiation phenomena on a principle of shock-wave propagation.) Working from his accomplishments in electrodynamics (e.g., the principle of retarded potential of propagation of radiation), Riemann proved that the cause of the manifest sound-wave track shown by a simple tuning-fork experiment, for example, is generated by a wave of the form of electromagnetic radiation. The rate at which the sound waves can be propagated in the atmosphere is the rate at which the air medium can be made self-transparent for propagation of an electromagnetic effect, which configuration cannot be assembled at speeds greater than the average velocity of the air molecules. On this basis, Riemann described the generation of such shock fronts as "sonic booms" in his treatise. The experimental demonstration of the unique accuracy of Riemann's treatise now shows that Leonardo was correct in principle in his views on the transverse-wave nature of the process of propagation of sound waves, and also in choice of method by which he developed his view on radiation propagated in the form of transverse waves.

In another instance, Dr. Steven Bardwell recognized, from viewing a museum exhibition of one among Leonardo's sketches of hydrodynamic turbulence, that Leonardo had obtained results not reproduced until the 1970s, by Dr. Fred Tappert et al., and that with aid of computer simulations! A researcher working on materials of the École Polytechnique and Leonardo, in Paris, Dino De Paoli, discovered that the method Leonardo had employed for these observations he had sketched was using water of different colors (!), by dyeing the water or suspending "tagging" material in it.

3. This is no exaggeration; the research has been conducted by methods including those appropriate to a major intelligence/counterintelligence investigation, under the direction of and with cooperation of relevant qualities of specialists. Begun approximately 1970, this continuing search on four continents, involving hundreds of persons in various aspects of the research, and exploring key archive materials previously left in large part untouched, has been among the most exciting and fruitful inquiries of which the writer has knowledge. To the point, the work thus far has been more than conclusive to the effect indicated in the text.

Admittedly, this report contradicts those legends and mere falsehoods or mistakes which have become popular in classroom and textbook. The so-called Leibniz-Newton controversy is an illustration of the way popular mythologies persist. It is documented that Leibniz submitted his first report of development of a differential calculus to a Paris printer in 1676, at the point of his departure for Germany. The document has been recovered, and Leibniz's work on the development of the calculus was already well known to the London Royal Society during the period of his 1672–1676 work in France. Newton's fluxions appeared a decade later, and although Newton's chest of laboratory papers survives to this day, there is no sign that he did much more on fluxions than coopt the work of (chiefly) Hooke and others. As Babbage's circle emphasized in a celebrated paper of the early nineteenth century, "Dotage and D-ism," Leibniz's calculus works, and Newton's does not, despite the combined efforts of Laplace and Cauchy to revise Leibniz's calculus in terms of a superimposed "limits doctrine." Nonetheless, the myth of the "approximate simultaneity" of Newton's and Leibniz's work is credulously asserted as fact or even zealously refought on Newton's behalf, to the present time. This is perhaps the most famous example of this sort, but is otherwise not exceptional in the sorry condition of textbooks today.

Part of the problem here is the substitution of textbooks for reliance on the student's working through primary sources afresh on his own power. Textbooks should be written either only by those reporting their own discoveries, or as an aid to a program of study of relevant primary sources. The trouble with textbooks, generally, is that they are written as a running series of glosses on formulations lifted out of context of original authorship. The pastiche which results often reminds one of a gossip-sheet columnist's running from one topic to another. "Now we come to So-and-So's formula. . . ." None of the actual continuity of work within specifics among the bitterly opposed factional currents is presented to the student, nor the nature of the profound differences in method and "axiomatic" assumptions of the contending parties. The "Cauchy-Riemann equations" are an illustration of the general sort of effect produced. Few leading figures in nineteenth-century mathematical physics were so entirely at odds with one another in method and ontological conceptions as Cauchy and Riemann, notwithstanding Cauchy's celebrated propensity for plagiarizing the work of his opponents, and then producing something of this as his original work, in slightly distorted form. To find an immediate Paris forerunner of Riemann's work, one must prefer Cauchy's immediate philosophical and scientific adversary, Legendre. The trouble is, this wretched method of passing along half-baked legends from Professor A to student B, who later becomes Professor B, and passes the slightly altered rumor to credulous student C, is so ingrained within the habits of educational practice that references to the actual work of the personalities and period referenced is received even among many esteemed professionals today as *lèse majesté*.

4. Since the Nobel Prize for economics was established, no candidate has been elected except that his "principal work" in the field flourishes with abominable incompetence, and also until the incompetence has been affirmed by some national catastrophe somewhere caused by adherence to the doctrine. Admittedly, in physics and chemistry, for example, the performance of the Nobel committee has been a bit more sensible. The authors of the "quark dogma" should therefore have been awarded the Prize for "economics."

5. On historical grounds, respecting some of the references within Panini's work, his writing should probably be dated to the 5th century B.C.

6. The current state of development of the Universe, or of the experimental phase-space of reference, should be denoted as of the order of some number N. Negentropic action raises this phase-space (for example) to order $N + 1$. This occurs *ontologically* within the continuous manifold. This is reflected into the discrete manifold as the addition of a new singularity. This is also reflected as a change in the metrical characteristics of action observed within the space of the discrete manifold. That metrical change is the experimental fact bearing upon hypotheses respecting the continuous manifold. (*Cf.* Riemann's 1854 habilitation dissertation.) Otherwise, if the universe were "infinitely extended" as physical space-time, the night sky would be brighter than the sun, since at every point the sky would be filled with the radiation from more than one star. If negentropic action is divided in effect as determined by order N, then this should be the determinant of the division of negentropic action against itself. Hence the conjecture outlined in the text. If this be so, then a relativistic change must alter the characteristics of physical space-time, such that the quantum values and speed of light are changed relativistically. This conjecture is supplied to illustrate what we ought to keep, as a nagging thought, in the back of our minds, as we proceed with mapping out experimental hypotheses for day-to-day investigations.

CHAPTER 6

Work versus Energy

Technological progress, mediated through advances in technology of production (chiefly), increases the productive powers of subsequent labor of operatives employing the capital goods (chiefly) of the preceding physical-goods output. This, and coherently radiated other changes in behavior of the society (economy), become the benchmark of reference for a new technological advancement.

This involves a two-fold increase in what is apparently the energy-content of energy of the system: first, an increase of the potential relative population-density; second, an increase of energy per capita. The energy increase per capita occurs both in increase of the content of the consumer-goods market-basket and the capital-goods market-basket. This energy increase implies a mathematical function premised upon rates of increase of *productivity* $[(S/(C + V)]$ and *capital-intensity* (C/V). The increase in activity-density per capita (e.g., energy-density per capita), is a correlative of increase of the potential relative population-density. Thus, it appears, the correlative of increase of potential relative population-density is an increase of both the per capita and per-square-kilometer increase of energy-flux density, as measurable in some term such as *kilowatt degrees per square meter,* a measure combining consideration of the number of kilowatts per square meter and the energy-flux density (as reflected by temperature equivalents) at which that energy is supplied. Better than kilowatt degrees were the standard of measurement supplied by a *coherent beam of electromagnetic radiation, of specified wave length and power transmitted* (e.g., a coherent beam of yellow light). The measurement of power supplied per capita

113

in this form, correlates with increase of potential relative population-density to provide the basis for a generalized, *hydrothermodynamic* function of increase of potential relative population-density. Such a function meets the need for *a general theory of mathematical physical economy.*

Such an approach subsumes development of knowledge in this matter along a trajectory passing through the successive work of Nicolaus of Cusa and Leonardo da Vinci, a trajectory subsuming also the work of such figures as Leibniz, Gauss, and Riemann. Education in economic science thus represents the student's "reconstructing" the internal history of that trajectory up to the point represented by the indicated general function. *That is both a curriculum and a method.*

The simplest symbolic representation of a function of increase of potential relative population-density is as follows. At each "point" in the discrete manifold construct a self-similar conical spiral. The increase of the circular cross-section of such a growing cone's generation by the self-similar spiral, is the measure of potential relative population-density. This is a measure of changes in mankind's functional relationship to nature (to the universe). Interpreted as a hydrothermodynamic function, it subsumes, functionally, the notions of energy required.

The increase of potential relative population-density, as the cited injunctions of Genesis require, and as the indicated conic function symbolizes this, is the definition of *work* coherent with *economic value.* This *work* is distinguished by the generation of the singularity by conic action.

The meaningful definition for a term "energy," in this context described, is, preferably, a self-similar cylindrical-spiral action. This we adopt as *the normalized form of energy.* Not-normalized forms of energy include a negative self-similar conical spiral of action, such that the singularity generated signifies "loss of work," or "loss of power to accomplish work." Not-coherent radiation of energy is included among the cases susceptible of being equated to that negative conic-functional form.

The mathematical prototype for the conversion of energy of the normalized form into work is modeled by Riemann's 1859 "On The Propagation of Plane Air Waves of Finite Magnitude."[1] The transformation of radiated energy into the conic form is the energy-work relationship.

Energy-flux density is normalized (to establish a standard of measurement) as a function of decreasing wavelength of coherent electromagnetic, cylindrical radiation. This includes the "properties" of retarded potential of propagation and induced self-transparency of the medium through which radiation is propagated. These subsumed features are associated with extension of the Principle of Least Action to the synthetic geometry of self-similar conic-spiral action in the continuous manifold.

It is to be stressed to the reader that the geometrical definitions of *work* and *energy* just outlined were adduced from the standpoint of increase of potential relative population-density (negentropy). This point emphasized, the same geomtrical functions for *work* and *energy* are obtained by applying the indicated contributions of Gauss, Riemann, et al., to Leibniz's application of the Principle of Least Action to the geometrical analysis of technology. In this latter approach, the reader should begin with the example of the heat-powered machine. The answer is obvious, in light of the discussion of conic and cylindric functions thus far. The case for electromagnetic action is also clear in all preliminary respects from the vantage-point of the coherence of Riemann's cited 1859 treatise in both Riemann's continuation of the Gauss-Weber work in electrodynamics,[2] and the posthumously published papers and lecture notes on this subject.[3] This leaves the matter of the case for chemical work-action and energy transport.

The fundamental ontological flaw embedded within

The transformations achieved through the use of heat-powered machines point to the invalidity of the Three Laws of Thermodynamics' rule of entropy.

chemistry ought to be rather readily recognized at this stage of our text: the implicit assumption that atoms are composed of smaller "elementary particles," which "particles" are, in turn, implicitly assumed to be more or less of the form of elastic solid bodies. Since the work of Professor Erwin Schrö-dinger, it has become more or less axiomatic that electrons are "particles" and "waves" at the same time, a discovery which inherits Schrödinger's study of the cited 1859 treatise of Riemann. The general drift is to the effect that an electron is a "wave-packet," not only mathematically but *also onto-logically*, a singularity of a hydroelectrodynamic process in the sense that the shock-front predicted by Riemann's 1859 treatise is the generation of an added singularity in what is implicitly also a hydroelectrodynamic process. More recent fundamental research, notably results obtained with plasma-focus experiments, are pointing to a fresh view of the evidence that all so-called "elementary particles" are also "wave-packets," ontologically as well as mathematically. In other fundamental experimental research, in the Soviet Union as well as the United States, diffraction associated with massed "elementary-particle" discharge (e.g., proton beams) contributes to the same view of the matter. This kind of result accords with implications of Gaussian derivations of elliptic functions, as we summarized highlights of that matter earlier. From this standpoint, not only elementary particles, but atoms and molecules, must be complex electromagnetic—hydroelectrody-namic—organizations. It appears not to be the case, as long as chemistry generally confines itself to experimental realms in which those ontological matters are not implicitly at issue, in which no significant difference in results is determined by preferring the solid-body view of elementary particles over the hydroelectrodynamic view. However, such a practice of chemistry must therefore exclude consideration of negen-tropic processes, such as the chemistry of living processes *as such*; chemistry in that form can be applied to biological processes only insofar as the characteristic transformations of living processes are not directly considered.

This implies that no geometrical model of *work* and *energy* could be derived from a chemistry which had not overcome the ontological fallacy indicated. This is usefully restated. Negentropy appears in chemical processes, defined as chemical processes, only as the phenomena of *life as such*. Insofar as chemistry bears the "hereditary" impact of assuming elementary particles implicitly to be elastic bodies, it is impossible to define the phenomena of life as such from the standpoint of chemistry. This problem is embedded in the axiomatics of chemistry, and the latticework of chemical theorems can therefore contain nowhere any experimental knowledge which might lead to discovery of the chemical nature of life as such as long as that experimental theorem carries the burden of the "hereditary principle" of the indicated ontological assumption. The problem is not that chemistry is insufficiently sophisticated; more sophistication would accomplish nothing on this specific point. The problem is elementary. All doctrines bearing the assumption of existence of self-evident solid elementary particles are analogous to an algebra consistent with the axiomatic assumptions of the self-evident existence of so-called real numbers; *all such systems are intrinsically entropic*. As Hamlet said: "There's the rub."

Fortunately, in measuring functions of work and energy associated with chemical processes, we are able to employ measurements which imply that chemical processes are electrodynamic in this respect. Until the indicated ontological fallacy is overcome, it appears that we have no choice but to assume that the significant work and energy functions of chemical processes are congruent with hydroelectrodynamics. Moreover, it appears that this is the point of departure which must be adopted in biology's studies of the characteristics of living processes as such.

These are the approaches which economic science must apply to mathematical physics, chemistry, and biology, insofar as we are considering the selection and effects of changes in technology incorporating productions of the research laboratory.

This requires economic science to dump the so-called Three Laws of Thermodynamics, and also those features of thermodynamics hereditarily congruent with such arbitrary postulates. The scalar, caloric notion of energy must be discarded, and with it the notions of scalar equivalence of *energy* and *work*.

We measure energy transport by the normal yardstick we have indicated above: coherent radiation of energy according to a cylindric self-similar propagation of a specified wavelength in the discrete manifold. This is the propagation of work done by a normalized form of conic self-similar function at some point of the spiral of the process of work (negentropy). The generation of work by transport of energy is the conic function of the form implicit in the cited 1859 Riemann treatise.

This is reflected in the practice of measuring the work accomplished to produce energy and comparing this with the work accomplished by application of that energy. The increase of the energy-flux density is the yardstick for measuring these relationships hydrothermodynamically. This method of analysis corresponds to the requirement that such processes treat economies as closed hydrothermodynamic processes (i.e., in the continuous manifold). Thus, we circumscribe what we identified earlier as "the curious phenomenon" of economic science.

NOTES

1. The English translation of this is by Uwe Parpart-Henke and Steven Bardwell, in *International Journal of Fusion Energy*, Vol. 2, No. 3, 1980.

2. Gauss and the Webers began assembling the state of the art

concerning electrodynamics during the 1820s. Unfortunately, as a by-product of the coronation of Queen Victoria in Britain, advanced scientific work at Göttingen was suppressed by the British-Hanoverian royal family. After this deplorable interruption, the work was resumed, and was continued by Riemann. A summary of Riemann's position in the development of electrodynamics is included in Carol White, *Energy Potential*, New York, 1977. That text includes as appendices translations of the Hattendorf publication of Riemann's lectures on gravity, electricity and magnetism at Göttingen during the summer semester, 1861, and also a translation of Riemann's 1858 paper, on the subject of a new theory for electrodynamics.

3. A matter arises in connection with the latter, 1858 paper, which merits attention at this juncture. When this paper was published in the 1876 Dedekind-Heinrich Weber edition of Riemann's selected writings, Weber appended a critical note:

> After the paper had been published after *Riemann*'s death, it was subjected to criticism by *Clausius* (Poggendorf's *Annalen*, Vol. CXXXV, p. 606), whose essential objection consists of the following.
>
> According to the provisions, sum
>
> $$P = -\int_0^t \sum\sum \varepsilon\varepsilon' F(\varepsilon - \frac{r}{\alpha}, \tau)d$$
>
> [summation of $-\varepsilon\varepsilon' F(t - \frac{r}{\alpha}, \tau)$—L.H.L.]
>
> has an infinitesimally small value. Therefore, by virtue of a non-infinitesimally small value that will be found later for it, the operation must contain a mistake, for *Clausius* found an unjustified reversal of the sequence of integration in the exposition.
>
> The objection appears to me to be well-founded, and I am of *Clausius*'s opinion . . . the most essential content of Riemann's deduction collapses as a result of this . . . [emphasis in original].

The criticism is fairly described as absurd, but yet illustrates precisely the fundamental differences in method between Gauss, Riemann, et al., on the one side and their dedicated adversaries, such as Clausius, Helmholtz, Maxwell, Boltzmann, et al. Algebraic constructions aside, the underlying point of Clausius's criticism is that he rejected the mathematics of a Riemannian continuous manifold, which is why their mathematics differ. Even so, careless gossip, such as Heinrich Weber's, has held up invaluable progress implicit in comprehending the importance of this and related aspects of Riemann's work on electrodynamics.

4. Professor Winston Bostick is in progress of producing a book on this and related results. Some of this material was presented by Professor Bostick at a private seminar in Leesburg, Virginia during early January 1984. Work in this direction by Bostick and his co-workers has commanded special attention in certain leading Soviet laboratories for years.

CHAPTER 7

A Chapter Dispensing with Monetary Theory

Most of what passes for modern expertise in economics is not unfairly compared to pulling your trousers down over your head as the first step in pulling them up over your legs. From the starting-point of Physical Economy's ABCs, as much of contemporary economics-textbook material as is worthwhile to know can be reduced to a week or so of study. It's not a diplomatic thing to say, but it's the plain truth. Accordingly, we devote a single chapter of this text to the supposed mysteries of monetary theory.

First, as to the general state of monetary theory today.

What passes for "economics" in textbooks and professional journals today is essentially nothing more than monetary theory. Some of the essential topics of Physical Economy are ignored, or, at most, explicitly ejected from the course. Insofar as contemporary academic economics touches upon topics of Physical Economy, the apparatus employed is bowdlerized bits and pieces of a rewarmed physiocratic dogma, or odd bits scraped from Marxist writers. As much attention of this sort as is given to topics of Physical Economy, all of it is subordinated to a monetarist dogma. "Buy cheap and sell dear" is the axiomatic basis of monetarism throughout; everything is considered from the standpoint of the fraternal association of fish peddlers and their bankers.

The specific fallacies of contemporary monetary theory are assorted into two complementary classes, both implicit in the "doctrines of morality" taught by David Hume, Adam Smith, and Jeremy Bentham. The first is identified by the slogan, "Magic of the Marketplace": the attempt to explain all facets of the economic process considered from the standpoint of price theory. This makes the attempt at description of real-life economic processes impossible to accomplish accurately, and monstrously complex in the failed attempt. The second principal source of incompetence of monetary theory is the effort to justify as valid economic practices various forms of usury, to appear to explain why these are indispensable features of the economic process as a whole. This makes the attempt at description even vastly more complicated and cumbersome.

Physical Economy permits us to avoid the first class of errors entirely. The principles of Physical Economy support long-established Augustinian teaching, that all forms of usury (usury in lending, usury in the guise of ground-rent, and usury in the guise of commodity speculation) are immoral and destructive of the general welfare. If these immoral and destructive practices are outlawed by policy of practice, the theoretical difficulties associated with accounting for their day-to-day effects are eliminated at the source. By aid of these two measures of instruction, the valid features of monetary theory are reduced in scope to principles which require no more than one chapter of an economics text.

In American history, monetary theory begins in fact with the Mathers' writings and Dr. Benjamin Franklin's (1706–1790) proposal to establish a paper currency for the English colonies in North America, based on the Mathers' work.[1] Monetary theory became well established under President George Washington, as is shown in Reports to Congress on credit and banking by U.S. Treasury Secretary Alexander Hamilton (1755–1804).[2] This was amplified by Mathew Carey (1760–1839),[3] and elaborated in greater depth by Henry C. Carey (1793–1879).[4] Key elements of this policy are embedded in Article 1, Sections 8 and 9 of the U.S. Constitution.

The elements of monetary theory are as follows.

The amount of money put into circulation, as wages and other money-income, is a function of those items of cost corresponding to energy of the system. The actual amounts put into circulation may vary from this ration of output in various ways, through price fluctuations, or through money flows through channels of Overhead Expense which have no functional relationship to the production cycle. Insofar as the production cycle determines payments, production's determination of secular growth of the money supply is determined as indicated. Production does not generate a ration of money supply adequate to permit purchases of the free-energy ration of output.

This matter we have just identified is sometimes referred to as "the buy-back problem."

The remedy for this deficiency is the power of government. To obtain circulation of money for purchase of physical goods corresponding to the free-energy ration, the government must either tax away money from financial flows through elements of Overhead Expense which are not economic—such as usury, ground-rent, speculative reselling, or the goverment must create money. Both measures may be combined into one.

The method by which a government should create credit is the issuance of gold-reserve currency notes of its Treasury, preferably as lendable sums circulated through the national banking system. The issues of money are placed into circulation through bank loans. Since these loans are predominantly secured loans, the value of the currency so circulated is backed by the security for these loans. The government is liable in fact for the percentile of total such issues of currency which may prove to be inadequately covered by security for loans so extended at some future date. The principal liability a government may expect to incur in this way, is from imbalances in foreign-payments accounts; since there is no international currency to cover this contingency—nor should one ever be tolerated by a sovereign republic[5]—balance-of-payments deficits on foreign account are settled by the Treasury through payments in monetary gold.[6]

That, in bare essentials, is a *gold-reserve monetary system*.

The best-known of the opposing doctrines of monetary policy are the *gold-standard system*, typified by the London-centered system of the late nineteenth century, and the present "floating-rate" form of the Bretton Woods (International Monetary Fund, World Bank, GATT, et al.) System.

In a gold-standard system, the U.S. Treasury would issue exactly one dollar in paper currency for each one dollar's worth of gold coin or bullion on deposit in the Treasury, or each private bank or banks authorized by governments of individual states of the Union would be authorized to issue its own paper currency to the extent one dollar of gold was held in reserve in the issuing bank, to the effect that any person presenting paper currency at the offices of the issuing agency could freely exchange that currency for its par value in gold coin or bullion.[7]

The gold standard limits the amount of currency in circulation to the amount of gold on deposit with the Treasury and/or banks authorized to make such issue of paper currency. When the United States was subjected to this arrangement, under the U.S. Specie Resumption Act of the late 1870s, the nation was plunged into protracted social crisis fired by deep and prolonged economic depression. During that period, and later, foreigners were enabled to buy up large parts of the real estate and other assets of the U.S. government and private U.S. citizens, largely at "dirt-cheap prices." Worse, since our shortage of gold bullion on U.S. Treasury deposit was depleted by the policies associated with the Specie Resumption Act, less productive nations than the United States, and private interests with gold holdings, were able to loot massively the federal government and our private citizenry, by purchases with paper currency for which there was no comparable backing in terms of supplies of physical-goods output available.

The crucial point to be emphasized, from the standpoint of monetary theory, is that the gold standard is worse than no issuance of paper money at all. The essential point is that there is no functional relationship between levels of output of physical goods and money in circulation. In the case of the outlined gold-reserve system, the essential backing for currency issued is not gold, but rather valuable physical assets, useful goods. Moreover, in a properly functioning gold-reserve system, the money supply is in approximate correspondence with goods in circulation. In a gold-standard system, the money supply is greatly below the level of goods offered for sale by production: hence economic depressions—often exceptionally severe depressions—are the correlative of the gold-standard system.

The effectiveness of the gold-reserve system depends upon the lending policies governing loans of currency issues. The following criteria are needed to ensure optimal effectiveness.

1) The only general economic application of loans of currency issues should be for either physical-goods-producing investments, or investments in development of basic economic infrastructure essential to physical-goods production. Other lending should employ loan of deposits of currency, specie, or bullion, as private savings with lending institutions.

Currency issues should be directed to investment in newly produced physical goods, preferably new capital goods, and should not be used more than temporarily, for brief periods of stimulation of a depressed economy, for consumer-goods-purchase debt. The currency issue must not be loaned for investments in second-hand goods of any kind, or for

*New currency issues should only be lent for investment in production
and infrastructure. Above: the Federal Reserve System's headquarters in
Washington, D.C.*

refinancing, or cover any part of Overhead Expense beyond
occasional bare minimums essential as marginal supplementary amounts of lending in loans principally issued for purchase of new capital goods for production of physical output
or essential basic infrastructure.

   The object is both to stimulate investment in physical-
goods production, and to ensure that the obligations of government implicit in the issuance of currency are secured by
investments which, in turn, are assocated with earning of
income through production of goods, by the debtor.

   2)   Preference in lending must be given to technolog-
        ically advanced investments in capital goods,
        weighted in favor of capital-goods production,
        and that weighted in favor of the machine-tool-
        grade portion of capital-goods production.
   3)   Preference must be given to loans which are both

preferred loans by the standards just cited, and also involve participation in lending of private savings deposited.

This third criterion of preference should be made to function in the following manner.

3a) Currency issues should be loaned at rediscount rates significantly below borrowing charges in the lending markets for private deposits, in the range of between 2% and 4% per annum. Private banks relending these currency issues are permitted to attach a small premium to the lending of currency issues. Thus, the private bank will secure the most favorable conditions by "averaging" some of its own lendable deposits in the same loan in which government currency issues participate. If this "averaging" is a condition for participation of loan of currency issues, the private bank has a double incentive for taking advantage of the arrangement: its competitive lending power is increased, as well as its efficiency of turnover of bank deposits plus capital; its own lending power, augmented so by participation of loan of currency issues, obtains the relatively highest rate of growth of income among potential private depositors in that private bank's market.

3b) The government fosters better its objectives, by drawing greater ratios of private savings deposits into preferred categories of investments.

The mechanisms are simple. A private bank submits a proposed loan agreement with a preferred category of investor to the relevant agency of the Federal Reserve System (for example), which acts for the Treasury in this matter. On approval of the loan by that agency, the Federal Reserve draws a check against the currency issue deposited with it by the

Treasury. This check is issued to the lending bank. The check is deposited to the account of the borrower in that bank; the borrower is then permitted to draw upon that account with checks countersigned by the relevant officer of the bank, against approved categories of purchases consistent with the investment purpose for which the approved form of the loan agreement specifies. The currency issued is thus circulated to the seller of the specified categories of goods, services, and payrollees. In this way, the currency issues are conduited to the purpose of circulating the free-energy ration of national output.

The gold-reserve feature of the system must reckon with two distinct but interrelated kinds of contingencies. First, to the extent that currency issues are used directly for purchase of foreign goods, this creates a liability against the Treasury. Second, the secondary circulation of the currency notes issued may be employed for foreign purchases, to similar effect.

This foreign contingency is managed by currency-exchange regulations. Disbursements to foreigners for import-purchases are made chiefly in the currency of the exporting nation, to the effect that the U.S. purchaser (for example) buys foreign currency through the national banking system with gold-reserve dollars (for example). This becomes de facto import licensing, since purchases of foreign currency are limited to the amounts of each foreign currency the national-banking system (including the Treasury) elects to purchase. The criterion followed by the national banking system is the nation's balance-of-payments position with each nation. This is supplemented by the (properly adopted) policy, that the U.S. (for example) will not settle foreign accounts imbalances with any nations but those with which it has a reciprocal gold-reserve arrangement.

The latitude for increasing imports is managed by promoting exports. In this connection, the government performs chiefly three roles. First, it promotes agreements which facilitate exports of hard-commodity categories. Second, it maintains import-export lending functions which serve in international markets of U.S. export financing according to the same principles of economic preferences employed to regulate lending of issues of currency notes domestically, with emphasis upon promoting capital-goods exports, as these principles imply should be the case. Third, the government, with cooperation of the national banking system, trades off deficits and surpluses in combined U.S. public and private obligations among assorted trading partners to keep liabilities and assets in foreign-currency positions in accord with both securing U.S. (for example) gold-reserve positions, and needs of government and private interests of the nation respecting international trade.

These matters are complemented by government's economic functions. Broadly, to the extent possible, government should limit its direct economic functions to development and maintenance of basic economic infrastructure of agriculture and industry. Insofar as possible, it is desirable that other economic functions be matters of private investments. In the area of government economic functions, in this case including U.S. federal, state, and local branches of government, the government either supplies basic economic infrastructure, or provides it through regulated public utilities. This includes water management, public transportation (ports, harbor facilities, major transportation such as railways, highways, highway freight, air traffic), energy production and distribution, natural-resources development and management, and municipal industrial infrastructure, including traditional municipal basic services.

It were prudent that government incur no accumulated medium-term to long-term debt for any reason but capital investments in such economic functions. The purchases by government for such functions should be of the form $(S' + C)$ in character, and in impact upon the economy. The rate of such purchases may be managed by loan of currency issues for such capital investments. This enables government to stimulate the realization of the economy's free energy, not only in net effect on level of purchases of physical-goods output as a whole, but also selectively. Since government has leeway for discretion in a large part of its adopted infrastructural investments, as to the year these are undertaken and the rate at which they are completed, prudent use of this leeway can afford selective stimulation to those areas of capital-goods output which require a margin of stimulus during a period. Yet, in so proceeding, government does not spend for anything but that for which it should spend in any case, and the impact of that spending is regulated as to net effects on the health of the economy as a whole. Additionally, by employing currency issues as a principal source from which to fund the debt portion of the capital investment, the debt levels and debt-management costs of government are maintained at the lowest cost.

The principal standard for policy-making in matters of monetary policy is the precalculated effect in terms of development of the physical economy as we have defined that up to this point. Thus, monetary policy is an extension and correlative of the mathematical function for Physical Economy. Government's part is chiefly to manage its own economic and monetary functions to the effect of shaping the total economic-monetary environment of private investment accordingly.

From the standpoint of economic science, the popular distinction between monetary policy and fiscal policy is a delusion. The government's power to tax, especially that of the national government, and the relationship of tax policies to management of the public debt, is immediately an integral part of monetary policy, with profound impact upon the direction in which the economy develops itself.

Taxation has a double function. It must satisfy the current payments obligations of government, but must also distribute the weight of taxation over the economy in such a fashion as to tax least heavily those activities which are relatively most desirable, and to tax most heavily those things which are least desirable. Again, the analysis of the principles of Physical Economy provided in this text is a general guide to policy-making.

For example, tax rates should fall most heavily on such undesirable activities as usury in all forms, and items of national Overhead Expense which are at the borders of immorality. Either wipe out sin, or tax it to the verge of extinction, Correspondingly, heavy tax burdens on household of operatives (for example) are both immoral and economically regressive in effects. Although ability to pay should generally be in proportion to the bounty obtained from the nation's provision of opportunities, the desirability of high rates of private capital investment pronounces it catering to foolish demagogues to tax high income punitively merely because it is high income. How the income is used is the moral and economic-functional distinction to be applied. If income is saved, and those savings invested or loaned to promote useful capital investments, as principles of Physical Economy define relative usefulness, it were prudent to provide some form of tax-investment credit for that portion of income, and thus to let the burden automatically fall with greater weight on the income of wastrels.

Respecting both the flow of credit through financial institutions, and flow of purchases from income, if one aspect of the economy is relatively starved, and another promoted by the effect of such differential rates of flow, that differential will shape the structure of the entirety of the national economy for better or worse over the period this prevails.

This touches upon a principle of natural law, as Cusa, for example, is a leading authority on law for modern civilization. The natural rights of each and all individuals is the proper definition of the term *equity* according to such natural law. The essential right of the individual is a *human* right, which is to say a right premised on the quality which distinguishes men and women from beasts: *the power of creative reason.* The development of the powers of reason in all young individuals, up through the level corresponding to modern technology, is a human right. The right, and obligation, of the individual to continue the development of those powers, is a human right. The freedom to employ those developed powers in some manner which renders an individual's having lived of durable value to society after that life has ended, is a most fundamental human right: otherwise, the value of man goes into his grave, like the value of a mere beast. It is the human right of each and all, that human life be regarded as sacred in principle of practice, and that that life be lived to such effect that its contributions to society shall be of continued benefit to humanity generally for generations to come. Wherever some other kind of designated right may conflict with this designated principle of human right, that other must yield; *that is the principle of equity under natural law.* No contrary definition can be tolerated under natural law.

Since the economy and the state are the instruments upon which the fulfillment of human rights for each and all depends, those functions of the economy and state which are indispensable for satisfying the principle of equity, also partake of the protection of the principle of equity. Wherever any other right or privileges may violate the rights extended to economic process and state by the principle of equity, the other is nullified to that degree.

For example, to cite a famous example of the principle of equity under natural law, if exaction of payment for debt from a debtor destroys a human life, or otherwise violates the principle of equity, the creditor must not obtain repayment on such terms, and if no alteration of the time and other terms of payment can remove the fault, the creditor's claims to payment are nullified under natural law: the Shylock doctrine.[8]

The principle of equity, as summarily described above, directly or implicitly defines all matters of public morality, in practice of government or of private institutions and private persons. The burden of responsibility for ensuring what is protected by this principle is in proportion to the relative power of the institution or person in the matter of equity at issue.[9] The ultimate responsibility lies with government.

Were it to be argued, that such a principle of equity lies outside the province of political economy's adopted subject-matter, this argument were simply shown to be both false and immorally so. Simply: the principle of equity is another guise for Physical Economy's definition of *economic value*: or, rather, the proof of this definition of economic value, by construction, given in this text, is the guise which the principle of equity assumes within political economy.

Hence, government has the moral right, and the moral obligation, to shape the impact of taxation upon society in the manner which best serves Physical Economy's principle of economic value, on condition that this application is also consistent with the principle of equity from which the principle of economic value is derived.

We have thus covered all of the essential points of a morally permitted species of monetary theory; any contrary theory is an immoral one, perhaps by intention, but assuredly in respect of consequences of its application to public policy. A brief review of the standpoint of Hume, Adam Smith, and Bentham, is sufficient to illustrate the distinction; the proof follows implicitly and clearly from the illustration.

The effort to justify a comprehensively immoral doctrine of public policy in Britain is most indebted to these three eighteenth-century figures. The doctrine in defense of such immorality was elaborated by Hume. The direction of his work to this effect was adopted in his Voltairean[10] *A Treatise of Human Nature* (1734), and elaborated as a more comprehensive dogma in *An Enquiry Concerning Human Understanding* (1748)[11] and *An Enquiry Concerning the Principles of Morals* (1751). Hume's doctrine of morals shaped directly the elaboration of the same doctrine by Adam Smith, in *Theory of The Moral Sentiments* (1759), and as the doctrine of "The Invisible Hand," in his *Wealth of Nations* (1776). Bentham's (1748–1831) chief works on the subject of political

Adam Smith

Jeremy Bentham

economy are his *In Defence of Usury* (1787), and *Introduction To The Principles of Morals and Legislation* (1789 edition referenced). The essence of the doctrine of political economy of these three, and others, is efficiently summed up by a passage from Smith's *Theory of the Moral Sentiments*:

> The administration of the great system of the universe . . . the care of the universal happiness of all rational and sensible beings, is the business of God and not of man. To man is allotted a much humbler department, but one much more suitable to the weakness of his powers, and the narrowness of his comprehension; the care of his own happiness, of that of his family, his friends, his country. . . . But though we are endowed with a very strong desire of these ends, it has been intrusted to the slow and uncertain determinations of our reason to find out the proper means of bringing them about. Nature has directed us to the greater part of these by *original and immediate instincts*: Hunger, thirst, the passion which unites the two sexes, *the love of pleasure, and the dread of pain*, prompt us to *apply those means for their own sake*, and *without any consideration of their tendency to those beneficent ends which the great Director of Nature intended to produce by them* [emphasis added].[12]

David Hume

Blind obedience to "original and immediate instincts," as defined from the standpoint of a pleasure-pain principle, is categorically subsumed under *irrationalistic hedonism,* the Biblical "original sin." Hence, the doctrine associated with Hume, Smith, and Bentham is an immoral doctrine, which, in its application by Hume, Bentham, et al. to matters of political economy, prescribed the "freedom" of such immoral conduct from any regulation by science or natural law. In short: Do what you *please* to whom you are able, and avoid the *displeasure* of whom you cannot resist. This doctrine, as continued by such figures of the British East India Company's Haileybury center as Thomas Malthus (1766–1834), David Ricardo (1772–1823), James Mill (1773–1836), and John Stuart Mill (1806–1873), are known alternately by the terms, "British nineteenth-century philosophical radicalism" or "nineteenth-century British liberalism."

The nature of such British liberalism is to be observed in its strictest, most self-conscious application in British colonial policy in India, as James Mill makes this conscious connection between British liberalism and its practice explicit.[13] It was under the influence of this doctrine, chiefly, that Karl Marx (1818–1883), working under the supervision of such British agents as Friedrich Engels (1820–1895) and David Urquhart,[14] elaborated his doctrine of "class struggle."

The question, as perceived by Marx and others, is what does Bentham's "greatest happiness for the greatest number" signify in the liberals' conscious application of their doctrine to practice? Bentham's own *Panopticon*[15] cannot be overlooked in this connection, since it represents a practical application of the doctrine of liberalism as deduced by Bentham himself. The historical precedent for such a dctrine of liberalism is such sources as Aristotle's (384–322 B.C.) *Nicomachean Ethics* and *Politics*, and such historical models as Roman imperial law and the self-described "oligarchical model" of Persian (Achaemenid) imperial doctrine of policy. On the basis of the latter classical precedent,[16] the doctrine under which British nineteenth-century liberalism falls is called *oligarchism*, the "oligarchical model."

At first glance, Marx's perception of British liberalism is not an inaccurate one. At first glance, the "greatest happiness of all" must be interpreted as of "all the British ruling class," specifically the British "Establishment" whose center of gravity during the indicated period was the British East India Company and Baring Brothers bank.[17] Yet, looking at the matter more deeply, we must admit that Bentham intended the "happiness" of all persons on condition that we also accept the presumption that races, and social classes within races, each have biologically determined differences in "original and immediate" instinctual needs, and that those needs are, in each instance, the needs inferred from the practice of the British East India Company and its accomplices toward each race and class within race. This was the composition and policy of practice of the Persian Empire, the Roman Empire, and the Assyrian and Babylonian empires before them, and the Ottoman, Austro-Hungarian, Russian, and British empires, later. This was also the policy of practice of that Swiss province called euphemistically the French Empire, and that Swiss-Hapsburg concoction called the Belgian Empire. The same is characteristic of the Dutch (East India Company) Empire, and so on and so forth. It is a version of the doctrine known today as "cultural relativism." Each race and class within that race, is awarded attributed special kinds of needs, not necessarily the same as other classes or races. The elaboration of such a doctrine is aided usually by interpretation of attributed "customs" and peculiarities of religious beliefs selected for such enterprises. In the end, Marx's attribution to the customs and religious beliefs of British liberalism is broadly accurate. The essence of the matter is the imposition of the *arbitrary will* of a "master class" representing a ruling race, upon the races and classes (or castes) in those races subjected to the rule of the dominant race's master class. This is the axiomatic principle upon which the elaborated ("cultural relativist") dogma of British nineteenth-century liberalism rests.

The earliest known literary elaboration of such a doctrine within England was by William of Ockham[18] A kindred doctrine was argued, chiefly against Peter Abelard ("of Paris," 1079–c. 1144) by Bernard of Clairvaux (c. 1090–1153). This reflected the Guelph (Welf) faction's ascendancy over the Vatican beginning with the accession of Hildebrand (Gregory VII, 1073), into the period of this controversy. Clairvaux's doctrine influenced Martin Luther (1483–1546), on divorcing faith from works. The principal origin of this doctrine of irrationalism was its importation from the Gnostics and Sufis of the Orient, largely through the influence of the Byzantine hesychastic movement conduited into Western Europe's religious orders through St. Catharine's of the Sinai and "Holy Mountain" at Mount Athos, Greece. The irrationalistic doctrine was revived in influence by the Black Guelphs' resurgence during the fifteenth and sixteenth centuries, as it has been promoted by that faction following the Guelph-Ghibelline wars of the thirteenth century. It was the Guelph faction, represented in England by the Stuart accessions and their sequelae: Francis Bacon (1561–1626), his personal secretary, Thomas Hobbes (1588–1679), and John Locke (1632–1704), are the immediate leading predecessors of Hume on this point. It was against this irrationalistic faction in Britain that the principal forces later leading the American Revolution founded chartered colonies in North America during the seventeenth century. It is to be emphasized that the fight against this irrationalistic doctrine was rather consistently a fight against the practice of usury by the faction promoting the irrationalists' dogma.

Smith's doctrine of the "Invisible Hand," derived explicitly from the dogma of irrationalistic hedonism in his *Wealth of Nations*, is coherent with the Second Law of Thermodynamics; Smith, and, more emphatically, Bentham's specifications for a "hedonistic calculus" (or, "felicific calculus") according to the same Humean principle, implicitly demand the version of "Ergodic Theorem" subsumed by the application of the Second Law to statistical gas theory ("statistical theory of percussive heat"). The doctrine of "marginal utility," as developed by John Stuart Mill, was based explicitly upon Bentham's "felicific calculus," as was the doctrine of the Vienna neo-positivists, typified by the prescriptions of John von Neumann for "mathematical economics."[19] Hence, the incompetence of the labor of contemporary academic economics must be justly identified as the "labor of immorality," the penalty of practising wickedness.

NOTES

1. "A Modest Inquiry Into The Nature and Necessity Of Paper Currency," 1729. Republished in N. Spannaus and C. White,

The Political Economy of The American Revolution, New York, 1977.

2. "Report On Public Credit" (1789); "Report On A National Bank" (1790). Republished in Spannaus & White, *op. cit.*

3. Carey's first references to these problems appear within his *The Olive Branch*, both the 1815 edition, and supplements published at points during later years. The principal reference is to Carey's contributions to *Addresses of the Philadelphia Society* (1819). These contributions are republished as an appendix in Allen Salisbury, *The Civil War and the American System*, New York, 1978.

4. *The Principles of Political-Economy* (3 volumes: 1837, 1838, 1840); *The Credit System* (1838); *The Harmony of Interests* (1851); *The Slave Trade* (1853); and the previously cited *The Unity of Law* (1872). Compare also Friedrich List, *The National System of Political Economy* (1841). These have been republished as part of an *Economics Classics* series by Augustus M. Kelley Publishers, formerly of New York, more recently Clifton, New Jersey. On this see also A. Salisbury, *op. cit., passim.*

5. For reasons made clearer by later parts of the chapter, the agency which controls a currency governs; supranational currency is supranational government.

6. Such payments are made only to foreign nations which maintain a gold-reserve system, and which are committed by treaty to reciprocity with the United States (in this indicated case). Actually, within the bounds of such a multinational treaty agreement to a gold-reserve monetary system, gold need not be physically transferred, but may be allotted to the account of the creditor nation while remaining physically on deposit in (in this case) the U.S. Treasury.

7. The system of currency unleashed by President Andrew Jackson (1829–1837), and his controller, President Martin Van Buren (1837–1841), is a parody of the gold-standard system. Jackson's tearing down the Second Bank of the United States, completed by 1832, and turning the nation's money supply over to private banking interests represented by Van Buren, caused the disastrous Panic of 1837. It produced rapidly a "classic"

bubble of the John Law (1671–1729) variety (France, 1716–1720).

8. Shakespeare's dramas are rich in case application of natural law. Otherwise, like the famous *Hamlet*, his great tragedies prefigure Friedrich Schiller's classic tragedies, in which the kernel of the "plot" is a principle of statecraft, subsuming issues of natural law. Schiller's writings on his dramas, especially on the *Wallenstein* trilogy, should be mastered by every serious economist.

9. Other, popularized usages of the term "equity" in law are not properly considered here. These have arisen in our national practice through the influence of British law, itself an echo of Roman law, in which the principles of natural law underlying our Constitution do not exist. St. Augustine, Cusa, Grotius (1583–1645), Samuel Pufendorf (1632–1694), and Leibniz on natural law, are the currents leading into the original design of U.S. constitutional law. See, for example, Grotius's influential *On The Law of War and Peace* (1625), the *Commentaries* (on the laws of Prussia) of Pufendorf, among his other works, and see Leibniz on Pufendorf's included errors on the subject of natural law. The writer was pleasantly surprised, but not astonished to find a copy of Pufendorf's commentaries prominently placed immediately behind the desk of the great Prussian reformer Freiherr vom Stein (1757–1831). Vom Stein, the leader of the Prussian reformers (Wilhelm von Humboldt, General Scharnhorst, et al.) associated with the Stein-Hardenberg reforms, was, like Humboldt, among the close collaborators of Friedrich Schiller (1759–1805), and thus a reflection of the American republican faction in Germany sprung out of Franklin's transatlantic conspiracy of 1766–1789, revived after 1815 by the Marquis de Lafayette, European head of the American Society of the Cincinnati. Among republicans throughout the world, into and somewhat beyond the 1815 Congress of Vienna, the natural law of Augustine, Cusa, Grotius, et al. was the natural law known to all. Hence, Miguel Cervantes' (1547–1616) *Don Quixote* and dramas, richly echoing natural law, as also Shakespeare, John Milton, together with the King James

Authorized Version of the Bible, shaped the legal philosophy reflected in the original composition of U.S. constitutional law.

10. The close collaboration between the Jesuits in France and the leading banking families of French-speaking Switzerland, as the continental center of reference for the Jacobite faction in Britain, and the circles of the British East India Company during the seventeenth and eighteenth centuries, and into the nineteenth. The published correspondence of Voltaire (1694–1778) is an excellent source of first clues to the extent of this network during Hume's travels in France, and later. Hume's philosophy developed under these specific influences in France and Switzerland, just as Smith's work in political economy depended largely on training by the same circles of Hume's.

11. The second edition of this work. It was Hume's work which prompted Immanuel Kant (1724–1804) to undertake his own *Critique of Pure Reason* (1781) and *Critique of Practical Reason* (1788). Kant, as evidenced by his attacks on Leibniz and defense of Newton, was leaning strongly toward British and Swiss versions of empiricism and romanticism during the 1760s (e.g., his 1764 *An Inquiry into the Distinctness of the Fundamental Principles of Natural Theology and Morals*.) However, the immorality of Hume's doctrine of understanding was more than Kant was willing to tolerate. *Cf.* Preface to 1781 edition of the *Critique of Pure Reason*, on "philosophical indifferentism," and the *Prolegomena* (1783) on the subject of Kant's general reaction to Hume's work. The anti-Leibnizian side of Kant shows in his "thing in itself" and related matters, and shows at its worst in his *Critique of Judgment* (1790) and his commentaries on the subject of aesthetics.

12. Except for addition of emphasis, the passage is as cited in LaRouche and Goldman, *The Ugly Truth about Milton Friedman*, p. 107. That book is the only available survey of the history of development of modern monetarism.

13. *History of British India*, 3 volumes (1817). That Mill's practice as an official of the East India Company was in accord with the teachings of Malthus and Ricardo is elaborated in his *Elements of Political Economy* (1821). From 1819 to 1836, James

Mill was the principal architect of British government in India, and hence clearly the principal author of the atrocities perpetrated according to the strictest application of British liberalism.

14. David Urquhart, whose influence Marx acknowledges in passing in several locations, was associated with the British Museum during that period, at which location his principal secret intelligence function was coordinating British operations inside Giuseppe Mazzini's Young Europe organization according to policy direction emanating chiefly from Lord Palmerston. He was, in effect, an immediate controller of Karl Marx during much of the 1850s and early 1860s, a fact consistent with the fact that Marx was a protégé of Mazzini's. (It was Mazzini who personally called the London meeting to found the International Working Men's Association, to which Marx was invited. When the decision was made to dump Marx, about 1869, it was Mazzini's Young Europe which conducted the operation to accomplish this result.) The British Museum also figures in the targeting of Marx and his daughter by that rogue Dr. Edward Aveling, the lover of theosophist Annie Besant, and the source of the false report that Marx dedicated *Capital* I to Charles Darwin. Aveling did propsose such a dedication to Marx, but Marx peremptorily rejected it. Engels, who defended Aveling when the latter was caught red-handed in repeated roguery, was of course much more sympathetic to the Huxley-Darwin circles than Marx.

15. 1791. The *Panopticon* is a design for a slave-labor prison, which the degenerate aristocracy of Lycurgan Sparta would have much admired. Hitler's Nazis, who esteemed themselves as modeled upon Lycurgus's Sparta, carried out Bentham's proposal in the form of the slave-labor concentration camps. The slogan emblazoned over the entrance to the Nazis camps, "Work Makes Free," is a usage of words fully consistent with nineteenth-century British liberalism's views on the proper "freedom" to be afforded to "undesirable classes."

16. In the letters from Rhodes to King Philip of Macedon, proposing Philip's alliance with the Persian Empire, Philip is promised kingship over a "Western Division of the Persian Empire," subject to the condition that he order the internal affairs of

that "Division" according to what the letters describe variously as "the Persian model" and "the oligarchical model." Aristotle's *Nichomachean Ethics* and *Politics* are the most detailed specifications of *oligarchical* principles of this species. Inside classical Greece, the oligarchical models included Lycurgan Sparta, Cadmian Thebes, and the temples of the cult of Apollo (Horus, Lucifer, et al.) at Delphi and Delos. The more general historical examples are the kinds of oligarchical empires indicated in the text.

17. The key figure was William Petty, Second Earl of Shelburne, "Lord Shelburne." Shelburne, Smith's master from 1763 on, and also Jeremy Bentham's master, was the leading political figure of the interests represented by the East India Company and Baring Brothers bank, and the behind-the-scenes controller of the government of William Pitt the Younger. Aaron Burr, who narrowly escaped conviction for treason during and several times after the American Revolution, was an agent of Lord Shelburne's circle, as in the case of Burr's establishing the Bank of Manhattan as a front for the Baring Brothers bank. It was the influential families associated with Burr in various treasonous undertakings who introduced Adam Smith's teachings on political economy into the United States. *Cf.* Anton Chaitkin, *Treason in America*, 1984.

18. Probably 1285–1349. The best-known modern exponent of Ockham's views was the Austrian irrationalist Ernst Mach (1838–1916), famous in science for the scurrilous attack he led against Max Planck (1858–1947), and also exerted some influence upon Albert Einstein (1879–1955). Among the most celebrated byproducts of Mach's influence was Sigmund Freud's (1856–1939) doctrine of psychoanalysis, especially Freud's so-called *metapsychology*.

19. In addition to LaRouche and Goldman, *op. cit.*, the history of the development of the doctrine of marginal utility is traced in Carol White, *The New Dark Ages Conspiracy*, New York, 1980.

CHAPTER 8

Wages and Population

The relationships between the increase of population and production of wealth are the subject of the third volume of Henry C. Carey's *Principles of Political-Economy* (1840). In Chapter 4 of this present text, we described summarily the principal subcategories of the census of households and their members indispensable for national income accounting. We do not wish to provide an updated reworking of the material covered by Carey; we limit our attention here to defining the principles which determine the necessary, functional relationship between increase of population and net wages or equivalent under conditions of technological progress.

In the indicated location of this present text, we assorted the members of households into categories and subcategories as follows.

Pre-Labor Force	Labor-Force Age	Older
Infants	Labor Force	First 5-year
Children under 6	Non-Labor Force	Second 5-year
Pre-Adolescents		Third 5-year
Adolescents		Older

We divided households according to the modal employment of labor-force members of households. We noted that there are ambiguities in attempting such a distinction, but emphasized that it is the shift of composition of labor-force employment which is of primary importance, such that a consistent method of accounting applied to the small ration of ambiguous cases will overcome the problems.

In the same section of this text, we subclassified house-

Figure 1

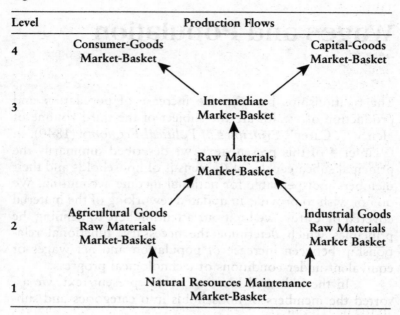

Level	Production Flows
4	Consumer-Goods Market-Basket ... Capital-Goods Market-Basket
3	Intermediate Market-Basket / Raw Materials Market-Basket
2	Agricultural Goods Raw Materials Market-Basket ... Industrial Goods Raw Materials Market Basket
1	Natural Resources Maintenance Market-Basket

holds of the Operatives portion of the labor-force by tracing the flow of physical-goods output backwards (see Figure 1). We closed the natural-resources maintenance cycle, by including basic economic infrastructure in the capital-goods market-basket, where it properly belongs.

We classified Overhead Expense categories of employment of the labor-force as shown in Figure 2.

Using only these three kinds of census distinctions, and applying the notions of the general mathematical function, we must interpret the effects which must occur, on grounds of principle, under either conditions of technological progress, or as effects of policy errors judged as errors from that standpoint of reference.

We begin by examining the ratios of the three principal age categories to one another, taking into account changes

Figure 2
OVERHEAD EXPENSE

Economic	Institutional	Waste
Services	**Governmental**	**Unemployment**
Science,	**Non-Economic**	
Engineering	Services	**Undesirable**
Teaching	Administration	Financial Usury
Medical	Police	Ground-Rent
. . .	Military	Commodity Spec.
Production[1]	. . .	Crime
Administrative	**Non-Governmental**	Immoral/Legal
Supervisory	Other Services[2]	Non-Functional
Prod. Mgmt.	Selling	Luxury
. . .	Financial	. . .
	Legal	
	. . .	

[1] Includes all categories of production flows, including transportation.
[2] Not elsewhere classified.

in the definition of the boundaries separating them from one another.

As the society advances technologically, the school-leaving age (or equivalent) tends to increase up to a point. We have today, a public-school educational requirement for technologically adequate levels of the labor-force generally of between 16 and 18 years (overlooking the accelerating deterioration of quality of curriculum and teachers during the recent twenty years or so, emphatically since 1967). Supplementary trade-school education means approximately two years added to that. A college bachelor's degree means a school-leaving age of 21–22 years modally. Terminal university degrees, an additional four years, approximately. Specialist education beyond terminal degrees, as in medicine or academic habilitation, an additional four to six years.

For reasons toward which we have pointed in the text thus far, the required elapsed time in educational institutions could be greatly reduced, in respect of quality of development achieved at the school-leaving age. If we uprooted the educational policies of John Dewey, and of the "de-schoolers" who followed his tracks, and restored principles of classical education according to Humboldt's principles, graduates of secondary schools would have competencies beyond those of recipients of university bachelor degrees today. This could include classical Greek and some foreign language undertaken by the present tenth-grade level, and a de-emphasis on algebra, in favor of synthetic geometry, at about the same grade level, leading to the comprehensive mastery of the elements of the mathematical physics of a complex domain by the point of secondary-school education. Presently, most of the years of public education today are being wasted by bad curricula, worse textbooks, and terrible lesson plans devised by teachers who are increasingly incompetent to teach. With the indicated, needed reforms in public-school education, the public-school graduate would have covered two, three or more years of the scope of present undergraduate education, and would have developed a learning capacity much superior to that possessed by students in higher levels of undergraduate education today. This implies that the total span of education required to qualify for a terminal academic degree could be reduced by about four years: reducing undergraduate education to about two years, and post-graduate degree work to a maximum of two to three years.

It is an error to assume that the accumulation of knowledge over successive generations signifies that each part of that accumulation must be swallowed one at a time, piece by piece. Progress in respect to fundamentals simplifies the comprehension of large areas of knowledge, to the effect that advancement of knowledge tends to lessen the educational time required to master subject-matters up to a fixed quality of knowledge. The design of curricula must be premised on this principle.

In summary of this immediate point: the school-leaving age does not increase indefinitely (in a well-ordered society); it approaches a maximum age-level "asymptotically." Generally, the school-leaving age should remain at the present modal level of between 16 and 25 years of age, with a very small margin of exceptions. However, within this indicated range of optional school-leaving ages, the level of required post-secondary specialist education varies chiefly as a matter of employment qualifications. Thus, we have reached the point (assuming necessary educational reforms are instituted) that the range of school-leaving age will not be altered; rather, the effect of further technological progress must be to shift the entire youth's school-leaving age closer to the 25–year-old level, as technological progress shifts employment prerequisites.

That point more or less put behind us, we turn attention to the change in age-level composition of the population since primitive hunting-and-gathering culture.

The principal consideration confronting us in tracing that aspect of technological progress is that the adult labor-force segment of the population must support the younger portion of the population up to the school-leaving age (or functional equivalent in more backward forms of society). Given the low productivities of backward societies, and the low life expectancies, child labor must be the rule. Not only do increased productive powers of labor require increase of the school-leaving age (or equivalent); such increases of the school-leaving age are not possible without corresponding increases in the productive powers of labor.

Given any average fecundity of households, and also given the per capita share of that household's market-basket, for each pre-school-leaving-age member, compare the amount of the market-basket which must be provided to sustain the infant, child, and youth members of that household each year. Now compare this with the per capita contribution to the average market-basket by the labor of the operatives of society. Restate this in terms of the number of labor-force operatives per household.

Restate this in terms of the total cost of the development of the total investment in a new entrant into the ranks of the operatives' component of the labor force, and similarly for entrants into the labor force more generally. We must take into account the costs of all entrants into the adult population. Apply this cost, first, to only that portion of entrants into the adult segment of the population who enter the labor force as a whole, and then also apply that total cost to only the percentile of the entrants into the adult segment who also enter the operatives' component of the entrance to the labor force. What is the pay-back to society of producing the operatives' component of the entrants to the labor force? We must proceed in this manner, since only the operatives' component of the labor force produces physical-goods output.

Next, deducting the Overhead Expense consumption of physical-goods output, and also the energy-of-the-system consumption of physical-goods output by production itself, examine the remainder per year per operative, and for the average number of labor-force operatives per household. Next, from this, deduct the annual market-basket of physical goods allotted to the adult members of the household. How many years must the operative work to "pay back" the investment in producing the entire population of entrants into the adult segment of the population each year?

Thus, for the hypothetical case, in which the productivity of operatives is treated as fixed, the "pay-back" potential is determined by the number of years the operative will labor efficiently. (Even in good health, the tolerable maximum pulse rate for physical exertion defines an estimable upper age level at which longevity no longer "repays" in terms of labor-intensive occupations.) It should be clear why a life-expectancy above seventy to seventy-five years, for a population whose labor force is composed about 50% of operatives, is

A declining birth rate, and shrinking labor force, generate pressures for euthanasia against the elderly and ill. Above: patient on renal dialysis machine.

needed to maintain the U.S. economy at standards of living considered decent today.

If we choose a modal retirement age for labor force members of 65 years, the required conditions of physical well-being at retirement-age employment require an implied number of retired-age persons in 66–69, 70–74, 75–79, 80– . . . , intervals. So, the cost of increased longevity is the sustenance of these age-group segments of the population, as well as the pre-school-leaving-age groups. We must re-compute the effective total investment in one active operative in the labor force accordingly.

Longevity, health, and other necessary conditions of such a population include medical costs, and so forth, which all must be assessed at the cost of producing the physical-goods output necessary to provide the full market-basket of goods and Overhead Expense items implicit in the indicated requirements. This approximately defines the term "necessary wage income or equivalent."

The reduction of wage or equivalent payments below this necessary level must have the kinds of effects on the characteristics of the population our construction implies. The attempt to lower wages below the necessary level, a trend in place in the U.S. economy since the aftermath of August 15, 1971,[11] leads to cuts in the quality of life of the pre-school-leaving-age and retirement-age segments of the population, together with cutbacks in quantity and quality of medical services provided per capita.

One cutback is reduction in the fecundity of households. This is obviously a means for reducing the real wages of the average household without a corresponding degree of decrease in the per capita market-basket share of members of households. Increase the rate of separation of retired persons from households of labor-force households, reduce the average level of existence of retirees so detached below that of average levels of labor-force households; in short, cut costs twofold: by decreasing payments to retired-age segments of the population, and accelerating the death rates among these segments. Also accelerate the death rate among persons below 65 years of age, by allotting medical services according to "cost-benefit" criteria: How much is it worth investing in this sickened person, measured against his tax payments and insurance-premium contributions over the remaining number of labor-force years?

In this sort of unravelling process, what begins as a cut in the birth rate leads toward euthanasia against both the retired-age segments, and, next, the seriously ill in the 50-to-65-year-old segment of the population.

Meanwhile, another development is tending to accelerate the drop in the birth rate and increase in the practice of direct and indirect euthanasia. The reduction in the birth rate becomes, within one generation's time, a corresponding drop in the number of entrants into the labor force. Even if the birth rate does not drop further, the chain-reaction results will include a lower number of entrants to the labor force 20–25 years hence than entered at the end of one generation's span leading to the first drop. If the birth rate continues to drop, the result will be much worse, of course. This describes the trends in the U.S. population and labor force (if only in broad terms of approximation) since the 1957–1959 recession.

First, we are becoming demographically an aged population: The size of the labor force is shrinking relative to the population of retirees, and the average age level of the labor force is increasing, especially in the relatively skilled and skilled-operatives categories. The aging among operatives generally is rising more rapidly than for the labor force as a whole, since the percentage of operatives within the total labor force is dropping, to the effect of increasing the percentage of prospective labor force entrants pushed into unemployment or marginal employment in labor-intensive unskilled services. Demographically, the United States, and a number of other leading "industrialized" (or, like Britain, "formerly industrialized") nations are dying nations, in the language of the demographer. A hundred years from now, German could have become a "dead language," for example, and the United States is moving in the same general direction.

We must stress again, that the drop in the percentage of operatives in the labor force is doubly critical. In fact, if we count all who should be seeking and obtaining employment today, we have approximately 25 million or more persons unemployed in the United States today. Since the physical-goods output required must be produced by the operatives' component of the employed labor force, the drop in percentage of operatives in the employed labor force, to approximately 21% during 1983, combined with the fact that there are about 25 million persons who should be added to the employed labor force, shows the reason for the spectacular cost-inflation of the recent eighteen years. The demographic picture shows what can be demonstrated in other approaches:

the United States' economy has been operating below true Physical Economy breakeven levels since no later than early 1980, and probably significantly earlier, as early as 1972–1974. The demographic picture shows how and why this has been occurring most clearly, most dramatically.

On the positive side of the matter, this foregoing discussion underscores the importance of meeting the necessary wage-plus-equivalent costs per capita fully for the smallest possible percentile of the employed-operatives component of the labor force employed in the stream of production of the physical-goods output, required either directly as physical-goods components of the market-basket of operatives' households, or as payments to Overhead Expense components of the consumer-goods market-basket of operatives' households. At the same time, to the same effect, the Overhead Expense component of the Gross Profit segment of physical-goods output must be prevented from growing as rapidly as Gross Profit; this includes, of course, the consumer market-basket requirements of households other than operatives'.

This cannot be managed without correspondingly rapid technological progress in productive powers of labor (economy of labor). This shifts the focus of our attention somewhat from the first chart at the beginning of this section, to the second.

In terms of national income accounting,

1) On condition that the necessary, demographically determined wage-plus-equivalent level per capita for households is satisfied,

2) $S/(C + V)$ and C/V must increase simultaneously, at relative rates implied by the general mathematical function.

3) This signifies an increase in the ratio of employment in capital goods to consumer goods production, as a function of increase of $(S' + rC)$, for the case that

r corresponds to the increase in productivity of capital goods through technological progress (as this point was elaborated in an earlier portion of the text).

4) However, this must be accomplished despite the effects of technological progress in requiring changes in demographic characteristics of the population, changes reflected as required increase in quantity and quality of goods contained in the per capita market-basket.

Referring to Figure 1, this requires an associated reduction in the percentile of the operatives' component of the labor force employed in raw-materials production, and shifting all of this relative decrease to employment in either capital-goods output, or intermediate-goods production. This must be assisted by strenuous efforts to collapse the Waste sector of Overhead Expense, checking the growth of Institutional forms of Overhead Expense, and checking inefficiency in growth of administrative portions of Economic forms of Overhead Expense.

At the same time, the absolute size of the labor force must grow. Technological progress increases the complexity of the division of labor in production of physical-goods output and related economic categories. This is reflected as *a lowering of the mean age level of members of the labor force, even while promoting longevity and increasing the retirement age.* This requires an increase in the birth rate, of course; but, there is the second matter to consider, the increase of the average school-leaving age in the 16–to-25–year-old interval, which means an increase in the social cost of developing a new entrant into the labor force, which, in turn, makes longevity improvements at a premium, and also raising gradually the modal retirement age (preferably by fostering opportunities for optional post-retirement employment, without forcing persons to give up previously contracted retirement rights). The wage-plus-equivalent costs must be determined as such a policy stipulates.

In government policy, this last matter touches upon taxation policy. During much of the post-war period, the U.S. government has forced a decline in the birth rate through taxation policy. Specifically, by causing increases in the deductions for dependent members of taxpayers' households to proceed much more slowly than the real rate of inflation, and at the same time taxing the same constant-dollar amounts of taxable portions of income at higher rates,[2] families with incomes at the level of skilled or semi-skilled industrial operatives have been rendered unable to afford to maintain the birth rate. In that sense, and to that degree, many millions of unborn Americans have been starved to death, in effect, before they were born, or in most cases, even conceived.

We must consider net wage-plus-equivalent income, not only of individual households, but of per capita income of members of households. We should consider the net, after-taxation amounts, first, for the existing populations of households, and, second, for the same households under conditions of normal birth rates. What a normal birth rate represents *economically* is to be determined by the methods indicated in this present section, up to this point. The latter enables us to determine the parameters of demographically necessary household income.

As we indicated, from a slightly different vantage-point, earlier in this text, the general direction of reform of tax policy must be to tax gains of usury to the point of extinction, while easing the taxation of initial portions of household income and providing tax-investment-credit "incentives" to savers whose savings are employed in improvement of physical-goods output. The most important feature of household income to be considered in lightening taxation in this sector is increase of the deduction allowed for each dependent member of a household. The minimum amount of tax relief to be supplied by these measures is to be determined by taking into account the required birth rate, as indicated just above.

Now, while retaining attention to the second chart, extend our attention to include the third of the three charts at the outset of this section.

Broadly, the rate at which a nation produces technological advances is a function of its scientific activity: the suitable employment of more and better-developed scientists and related professionals in producing science and developing its discoveries into forms suited for application to production. The rate at which technological progress is produced is, in first approximation, a reflection of the number of scientists and related specialists employed in research-and-development functions, per 100,000 employed operatives. For the United States presently, the target for this should be about 5% of the labor force, including skilled operatives employed to assist the professionals.

This brings us to the policy question: How is this research-and-development activity properly interfaced with production? We have already specified that the benefit of technological progress increases approximately in proportion to increase of capital-intensity. We emphasized that this is the case insofar as technological advancements are focused upon improvements in the production of capital goods (or, in the rate at which capital goods of constant quality are produced). This leads our attention to the special subcategory of capital goods, capital goods employed in production of capital goods. Broadly, a large capital-goods sector, including a relatively large machine-tool-class subsector, and with high rates of capital turnover in the latter subsector, and a fairly high rate of capital turnover in the category as a whole, is the correlative of a higher rate or economy of labor in the economy as a whole. Such, generally speaking, are the priorities.

This should be examined from another vantage-point, the principle of technology. Research and development must

The proportion of scientists and technicians in the labor force must grow to about 5% in the United States. Above, the U.S. Space Shuttle Columbia on its second test flight on November 12, 1981.

look at advances in the machine-tool sector in a twofold way:
1) the technological advancement in the machine tool, itself;
2) the technological advancement imparted to the capital goods
produced by this machine tool, an advance inherent in the
technological improvement incorporated in the machine tool.

For example, let us imagine any standard modern machine tool, of the sort used for cutting, shaping, surface treat-
ing, and so forth. Let us redesign this machine tool, employing
the same principles of design in every feature, except an
embedded complex which substitutes the use of a laser for
the specific function central to the machine earlier. The entirety of the advancement in technology of such a device is
located within that inserted assembly—although the entire
machine tool is indispensable to "deliver" the embedded part
in which the technological improvement is located.

The same principle is to be observed in the division of
labor in the productive process as a whole. A plumber, or
"steamfitter," employing no recent innovation in technology,
participates in installing a technologically advanced process;
since the plumber's action is indispensable to the functioning
of the process, the plumber's activity is participating in the
delivery of the technological advancement to the productive
process as a whole. Similarly, those who effect such innovations, or contribute in some essential way to their realization, drink cow's milk, consume grain, and so forth at
breakfast; although these breakfast items include no fundamental technological transformation in the design of cow's
milk, grain, and so forth, they are necessary to a process
through which technological progress is mediated, and so the
activity of the farmers, et al., in bringing those items to the
breakfast table, is participating in the delivery of technological
improvement in the particular industrial plant we might imagine for this case. Industrial products which catalyze economy
of labor in agriculture, including increased yields per hectare,
are a technological advancement in agriculture's economy of
labor, and are thus transmitted back into the industrial sector

of the economy through economy of labor, the which is transmitted back into the industrial sector through economy of labor effected in production of agricultural produce; as Alexander Hamilton showed at some length, with his report to Congress "On the Subject of Manufactures," Level 2 of the production process has shifted some of its ration of labor to the industrial sector.

An auto mechanic, performing exactly the same procedure on two automobiles in the same condition, contributes more or less (economic value) to society, according to the relative usefulness of the operators and passengers associated with the vehicle. Insofar as the auto is used entirely by a pimp, the mechanic's labor has negative economic value, whereas the work done on the auto required by a poorly paid, but essential, unskilled industrial operative and his family is positive in some relatively greater degree, according to the degree of contribution of technological progress, directly or indirectly, by the production process in which that operative is employed, or the future role, as operatives, etc., of pre-school-leaving-age members of his household. Similarly, the mechanic's work on the vehicle which transports the wealthy official employed in income of financial usury, ground-rent, or commodity speculation, has a negative economic value, like the case of the pimp belonging to the same category of Overhead Expense. Everything consumed by households whose income is from usury, prostitution, gambling, and so forth, is transformed into a negative economic value, such that that portion of the labor consumed in producing such goods is transformed into a negative economic value.

Any physical product, such as a machine tool, is an echo of the social division of labor in the society as a whole. The product, examined in the light of its process of production, is an echo of the demography of the entire society, that society's demographic characteristics. These connections are implicitly measurable backwards from the product situated within a particular productive process as a whole, to the population of households. Correspondingly, *the activity of every individual person in society has an implicitly calculable universal significance for the present and future of that society as a whole.* That value may be positive, negative, or null, and positive or negative in relatively greater degrees. Usurers, gamblers, criminals, drug-runners, and so forth have an existence which is negative for society as a whole, and this generally in approximate proportion to the level of income they receive from society. To that same degree, members of households dependent upon such sources of income, also have a corresponding negative value as persons in the present and future history of mankind as a whole. The same is implicitly the case for those persons whose characteristic social activity is gossiping, lying, cheating generally, down to the scale of the disloyal Judas. *For better or worse, all and each among us is a person of universal importance.*

Starting from the activities of scientific research and development, we must trace through the productive process, in each step, the localized change in technology incorporated in both the product and its application which embodies that change in technology. The machine tool in which that change is an embedded feature, must be designed to transmit the effect of that change as improved technology in the produced capital good, and the mathematical definition and analysis of technology is the same for the capital good produced with aid of the improved machine tool, as for the improved machine tool itself. The same analysis is to be performed respecting the employment of the capital good in production more generally. The relationship of this technological advance, so traced as transmitted, to the improvement of economy of labor in the society as a whole, closes the cycle. In this way, *the measurable advancement in technology, measured according to a Gauss-Riemann improvement of Leibniz's definition of technology (Principle of Least Action), has a measurable, causal connection to the resulting rate of increase in the productive powers of labor, and rate of economic growth.*

An advanced and relatively large machine-tool sector is a priority for upgrading capital goods as a whole, such as this boring mill, being applied to a closure head disc for the nuclear Fast Flux Test Facility.

That is the kernel of the LaRouche-Riemann method.

Thus, the demographic characteristics of households, and changes in structure of the division of labor, are changes directly to be correlated with the relative degree of negentropy, or entropy, of the social-productive process. The increasing complexity required in the social division of labor, by technological progress, is to be viewed as an increase in the species of singularities in a negentropic self-development of the productive process.

It is a corollary of this, that shifts in the composition of activities within society, represent an upward or downward shift in the economy, as the shifts in social structures correspond to negentropic or entropic changes in social structure. By forecasting the changes in composition of employment and income resulting from adoption of a policy of practice in taxation, credit, and so forth, we may determine whether those policies are intrinsically beneficial or regressive.

Our task today—for the United States, for example—is to discover the social composition of activities of households' members generated by adopting the variety of "science-driver" policy implied here.

1) Five percent of the total labor force employed in scientific research and development functions, centering this function upon mastery of a) controlled thermonuclear fusion and related matters of organized plasmas of very high energy-flux density; b) coherent radiation of very high effective energy-flux density, including lasers and "particle beams"; c) the principles of *living processes as such*, a fundamental revolution in biology reordering the definition of chemistry. The work in all aspects of research and development, must reflect advances in both technology and fundamentals of all scientific knowledge accomplished on the three indicated frontiers.

2) A goal of bringing the Operatives' component up to at least 50% of the properly calculated total labor force as rapidly as possible. This must increase the quality and magnitude of the per capita consumer-goods market-basket without increase of the percentile of the Operatives' component applied to production of that market-basket. The greatest

part of the expansion of Operatives' employment must be concentrated in capital-goods production, with a large relative increase of the proportion of machine-tool-level capital-goods production within capital-goods production as a whole. Level 2 production must tend to decrease as a percentile of the Operatives' component of the employed labor force.

3) Wages policy, including taxation policies, must focus on the fostering of the required changes in demographic characteristics of the population, as indicated above. This includes wage equivalents such as reforms of education, and proliferation of libraries, museums, and the kinds of cultural life coherent with a classical program of Humboldt's general type in education.

4) A high rate of export of capital goods to "developing nations" and other foreign customers must be fostered. This must be seen as contributing to economy of labor in the products we import from abroad, and in fostering a high rate of growth and capital turnover in our machine-tool sector and capital-goods sector as a whole. The higher the rate of capital turnover in capital-goods production, within the setting of not less than 5% of the labor force employed as specified in Point 1, the higher the rate of technological progress within the U.S. economy; the increased margin of turnover accomplished by capital-goods exports, increases the rate of technological progress's assimilation into all categories of capital goods produced for combined domestic and foreign use.

NOTES

1. On and immediately following August 15–16, 1971, President Richard Nixon instituted a program sold to him by a team of

spokesmen led by Treasury Secretary John Connally. The program's promotion was mediated through Undersecretary of the Treasury Paul A. Volcker (since September 1979, chairman of the Federal Reserve System), and had support from the liberal Democrats in the Congress responsible for monetary affairs. (The State Department was used as a channel for developing a steamroller in support of these policy actions.) There were two aspects to Nixon's decisions of that period: 1) he destroyed the international gold-reserve monetary sytem, and plunged the world into an inflationary spiral of "floating-rate" money, the cause of the present international debt crisis; 2) he began a process of drastically lowing both net wages of households (through the phased austerity programs of 1971–1972), and the rate of investment in production of physical goods. These effects were monstrously aggravated by the petroleum crisis, caused chiefly by operations of Henry Kissinger, of 1973–1974.

2. This has been described by economists and others as the "inflationary tax dividend." Inflation makes the per-dependent tax exemption worth less, in constant dollars, which means that a larger part of the total income of the household is taxed. However, since money-wages must increase, to keep pace with inflation, the taxpayer is pushed into a higher tax bracket; therefore, for the same constant dollar income, the taxpayer is taxed at a higher rate, year after year, and the total percentile of household income taxed at this higher rate is increased. So, inflation automatically increases the percentile of household and other income which is taxed, and this taxed at increased rates: "the inflationary tax dividend."

CHAPTER 9

Basic Economic Infrastructure

In a study of U.S. post-war investments in basic economic infrastructure, a team led by Uwe Parpart-Henke discovered that the closest statistical correlation to be met in economics is between rates of improvement of basic economic infra- structure and increases in productivity of labor.[1] Within ap- proximately twelve months after an increase of investment in basic economic infrastructure, there is a corresponding in- crease in the productivity of labor. If one lays the two charts on top of one another, shifting the chart for productivity back by twelve months, the two curves are almost identical.

Broadly, the United States increased the rate of in- vestment in improvement of infrastructure into the mid-1960s. The rate dropped after that point, but the total investment in infrastructure increased, at a dropping rate of growth. The total investment in combined improvements and maintenance of infrastructure reached a post-war peak during 1969. After that point, expenditures for combined improvements and maintenance of infrastructure have been below the "break- even" level. Today, to restore U.S. infrastructure's condition of maintenance approximately to levels of 1970, not less than $3 trillion (in 1983 dollars) would have to be spent for this purpose alone.

Traditionally, the responsibility for building and main- taining infrastructure has been that of government. Govern- ment has fulfilled this responsibility in assorted ways: 1) Direct expenditures by either federal, state or local governments for constructing and maintaining improvements of infrastructure;

2) Federal or other governmental corporations, such as TVA, port authorities, and so forth; 3) Regulated public utilities 4) Regulated private facilities of interstate or intra-state commerce, including public transportation and communications. Of this, a large chunk is in the form of direct outlays of budgeted Expense and Capital outlays of government (the first case listed above).

During this period, since 1970, but emphatically since 1973–1975, governmental expenditures in these categories have been reduced at an accelerating rate, especially if this is viewed by the yardstick of officially estimated constant- dollar values. If the true rate of inflation is considered, significantly more rapid than the "politically adjusted" official estimates, the shortfalls in maintenance of infrastructure in these subcategories of infrastructural outlays better approximates the physical decay which has actually occurred during the indicated interval.

With this in mind, reflect on the question: Where are the costs of decaying infrastructure reflected in the National Income accounts of the Gross National Product accounting system? In large part, they are unreported, and ignored. This implies that the national product (e.g., value added) of the United States during the 1971–1983 period has been overstated by as much as $3 trillion (in 1983 constant dollars) on this account alone. (We must lower this perhaps, to reflect elements of shrinkage of infrastructure actually reported in National Income accounts by private taxpayers, public utilities, and so forth.)

This means, that if the charges which should have been listed for depletion and depreciation of infrastructure had been included in public and private accounting practices, the margins of gross profits for combined private and governmental economic activities during 1971–1983 may have been overstated by some very large amount in the order implied by the estimated $3 trillion, 1983 constant dollars, deficit in infrastructure! In other words, these unreported costs of de-

A $3 trillion deficit in U.S. infrastructure spending? Above: Bridge disaster in Hartford, Connecticut.

pletion and depreciation should have been added to the costs of the market-baskets of capital and consumer goods for the 1971–1983 period.

About three decades ago, a group of raiders seized control of the New Haven Railroad (in New England). By curtailing expenditures on maintenance for roadway, rolling stock, and so forth, the paid-out costs were reduced greatly per dollar of railway revenue. One-time profits of asset-stripping added nomimal improvements in earnings to reported financial performance per unit of outstanding equity. On the basis of the price-earnings ratio, the stock's value zoomed; the raiders unloaded their stock holdings at a very substantial capital-gains profit, leaving a ruined railroad behind them as they departed.

That is the model for what has been done to the U.S. economy as a whole since about 1966, especially since 1971–

1974. It is not a new trick; by the means of bankrupting Jay Cooke at the beginning of the 1870s, and the introduction of the Specie Resumption Act, a similar process of looting was unleashed, the looting of railways a prominent feature of that process of the 1870s and 1880s. Many great American fortunes were made, in consort with British and other foreign looting of the U.S.A., by these means, during that period and later. The looting of the New Haven Railroad was, therefore, already an old trick at the time it was unleashed. Since 1966, especially since 1971–1974, this kind of looting has been deployed vastly against both infrastructure and basic industry.

Go back to 1763, to the time of the long carriage ride during which Adam Smith received from Lord Shelburne instructions for the destruction of the economies and limited self-government of the English colonies in North America. From that point onward, through 1863, the British Establishment, centered around the British East India Company during most of that period, was determined to destroy the United States of America. In aid of this policy, the Establishment faction of Lord Shelburne's circle enjoyed collaboration from a force within English-speaking North America: the Tories. This Tory faction, associated with Aaron Burr during the entire period to the end of Burr's life, had two broadly defined components. One group of Tories left the United States (some returning later); another group constituted the "stay-behind" networks of leading Tories. This included, chiefly, families linked to the British and Dutch East India companies in New York and New Jersey, and allied families of New England, including names such as Russell, Cabot, Lowell, Higginson, Peabody, Perkins, Cushing, and so forth.[2]

These families were behind the Jacobin insurrections of the 1790s, behind a Burr-centered plot to destroy the United States in 1800 and 1804, were caught in secessionist conspiracies in 1807–1808, were caught in massive treason during 1812–1814. During the 1780s, elements of this tightly intermarried collection of families were partners with the British East India Company's African slave trade, and beginning in 1790, were partners of the East India Company in the China opium trade. Together with British intelligence and Swiss and Jesuit interests, these same families organized the Civil War, beginning in the 1820s. They created the Abolitionist movement at the same time that they created the Confederate slaveholders' seccessionist conspiracy in the Carolinas: their purpose, as Democratic Party "king-maker" August Belmont also confided in his personal correspondence, was to split the United States into several parts.

This was the current of British agents of influence who collaborated with British Secret Intelligence Service agents such as Sir John Robison, beginning 1796–1797, in efforts to destroy the United States from within.[3] This was the faction which promoted the influence of Adam Smith's *Wealth of Nations* within the United States, as a leading feature of the effort to destroy the United Statees from within. These were the internal forces, within the United States, who controlled Presidents Andrew Jackson, Martin Van Buren, James Polk (1845–1849), Franklin Pierce (1853–1857), and James Buchanan (1857–1861).[4] With the defeat of their confederates, including Judah Benjamin (1811–1884)[5] and the Louisiana Slidells, the same families profited from the assassination of President Abraham Lincoln (1861–1865)[6] to unleash the looting of the states under federal military occupation, greatly augmenting the wealth they had accumulated from such noble enterprises as the East India Company's African slave trade and China opium trade.[7] They employed their wealth, in cooperation with London-centered foreign forces, to bankrupt Jay Cooke (1821–1905), and to bankrupt the United States through the passage of the Specie Resumption Act.[8] They pushed through the Federal Reserve Act, with aid of both their tool Teddy Roosevelt,[9] and their President Woodrow Wilson.[10] They control leading universities in the United States, leading liberal news media, major entertainment media, and most book publishing. They are the "liberal Eastern Establishment," popularly identified with a U.S. branch of the London Round Table organization first established as the National Civic Federation, and today the New York Council on Foreign Relations. They are what President Franklin Roosevelt (1933–1945) occasionally labeled "the economic royalists." They are sometimes called "the patricians," and have not infrequently hired writers to produce books and articles painting them in the image of the patricians of ancient Rome, the "bluebloods," the "families" constituting a wealthy American "aristocracy." They are *oligarchs* in the strict sense of the term, as we identified that earlier in this present text.

They are still attempting to destroy the federal constitutional republic of the United States. Exemplary: Pamela Churchill Harriman, wife of the former Ambassador to Moscow, Undersecretary of State, and New York Governor, Averell Harriman, is the sponsor of a faction she finances within the Democratic Party, a faction explicitly dedicated to rip up the Constitution of the United States, and establish a parliamentary system modeled upon Britain's. The Harrimans have been the leading racists in the United States throughout most of the present century; the eugenics movement is controlled by the Harriman family to the present date. Not only was Averell Harriman early a booster of Italy's fascist dictator, Benito Mussolini; at a 1932 meeting of the New York Museum of Natural History, a center of eugenics and related dogmas, the Harriman family joined in praising Adolf Hitler's Nazis for the Nazis' "racial hygiene" doctrines, doctrines virtually identical with those promoted as "eugenics" by the Harrimans.[11] "Liberals? 'Liberals' supporting not only fascism, but also Hitler's racial-hygiene doctrines?" It is sufficient to refer to our summary of British nineteenth-century liberalism, earlier in this present text.

Although these families have engaged in industrial as well as financial oligopolies, in their oligarchical philosophical outlook, they have been avowed Malthusians ("Social Darwinists") long before they and their foreign confederates of

The Third International Congress of Eugenics in 1932 at New York's Museum of Natural History beat the drums for Hitler's policies.

kindred oligarchical outlooks, unleashed "neo-Malthusianism" during the autumn and winter of 1969–1970. They have been the force within the United States behind the drive toward a "post-industrial society." Therefore, we must not delude ourselves that by rushing to these circles with proof that the destruction of U.S. infrastructure has been a disaster, we would persuade them to discover the error of their ways.

Frequently, the effort has been made to explain this or other, related features of the policy influences of this "liberal Establishment" in terms of "conspiracy." There is a large amount of conspiracy afoot in connection with the *implementation* of such policies. The conspiracies exist, but most of the offered explanations of the *why* and *how* of the conspiratorial features are made absurd by the writer's or speaker's efforts to explain the process in terms of simple greed, or something of that sort.[12]

The members of the "patrician families" themselves form a tight social stratum within our national life. They send their progeny to certain private schools and universities, within which the status of being scion of one of the "families," as distinct from plebeian attending the same institutions, is implicitly understood, and the understanding made policy of practice. The same implicit understanding pervades the clubs, fraternities, secret societies, and so forth which are approved for progeny of the "families." This extends to an approved set of churches, within a spectrum of approved religious denominations. It extends to financial institutions, and a roster of approved law firms, and so on and so forth. The implicit understanding is quite efficiently identified by the pronouns "we" and "they," the pronouns of oligarchical varieties of class-consciousness. All of this is associated with a sense that "we" share a different philosophical world-outlook than "they."

Over the period of about two centuries, during which this "liberal Establishment" has developed within the United States, the detailed features of generally accepted beliefs have undergone changes which have some outward features of paradigm-shifts. Yet, the underlying paradigms—the axiomatic features of generally accepted outlooks—have not changed. It has the appearance of changing "fads" in manners, morals, and concrete policy guidelines. It represents, in these respects, an evolving subculture, an evolving oligarchical subculture. This evolving subculture shapes the criteria of personal judgment within the overwhelming majority of the progeny of the "families" over successive generations. It is this mind-set, so determined, which governs the individual and collective behavior of that class, most emphatically in matters bearing upon the cultural, social, economic, legal, and foreign policies of the United States as a whole.

Conspiracy, therefore, is not the source of policy shifts this social class imposes upon the United States. Conspiracy is merely a means for coordinating and implementing what the currently evolved state of philosophical world outlook among the majority of the class's elders demands more or less "instinctively."

The appearance of "conspiracy" is relatively most pronounced one level below the class itself. Like the oligarchical families of Europe, for example, the families of the liberal Establishment keep an eye out for usable plebeian talent. The manifest policy of practice on this account appears to be an "instinctive" sense that "plebeian talent" ought either to be coopted or destroyed. Although "plebeian talent" includes "useful ruffians," in respect to the point under consideration in this portion of our text, we are speaking of plebeians of the professions and administrative upper echelons, plus a "useful politician" or two. The preferred sort of plebeian talent is that selected early, during or after adolescence, from populations of approved lists of schools, universities, and so forth. Potential youthful recruits are selected, the lists culled, and the closely scrutinized potential talents surviving the selective process are "groomed" up to the level of their estimated capabilities for usefulness. The feudal aristocrat's court is not to be overlooked as a model for the policy of practice involved.

Hence, in the administrative life of government and private affairs, there are distributed somewhat influential individuals who, to one degree or another, owe their existence to the "families." It is in the coordination of deployment of all or portions of this "talent" to concerted effect, that the appearance of conspiracy proper is most conspicuously generated. These "talented" poor devils—having, in a manner of speaking, sold their souls to the devil—reciting pat formulations more or less fanatically, with no visible resident behind their empty eyes but the imposed will of their owners: these are the apparent conspiracy. Generally, the families as a whole remain more or less in the background. They need do no more than agree that "something ought to be done about that" to set the process into motion.

For most persons in society, including leaders of industry, leading political figures, and so forth, the power of these families "gains respect." In that fashion, the families became "very respectable." "One does not take the 'families' head-on. One doesn't take the Establishment head-on." So, the policy directions dictated by the families become usually the policy of practice of the nation.

Was the destruction of the U.S. economy's infrastructure planned? In the sense indicated by discussion of the "families?" Yes, more or less precisely so.

As to the position of infrastructure within the economic process as a whole, it is sufficient to situate the points being developed in this section in the context of our hypothetical consolidated agro-industrial enterprise. Except for that aspect of the infrastructure which pertains exclusively to functions of households, infrastructure is a capital investment in the productive process: water management, transportation, production and distribution of energy supplies, communication, and the urban infrastructure indispensable to the production and distribution of physical goods output. Insofar as households supply the labor force, the modern urban-industrial complex as a whole exists for the convenience of the production of physical goods. The households constitute the "labor market" indispensable for industrial development, and the structure of a well-designed urban center is properly rooted in the topology of movements of members of the labor force to and from places of employment, plus movements of children and youth to and from places of education.

It is most fruitful to look at the proper design of urban centers on Earth from the vantage-point of developing urban centers on the Moon and Mars during the coming century. This serves a double purpose. In the lesser, but not unimportant aspect, the adoption of that benchmark encourages us to clear our minds of assumptions rooted in our habits, as associated with urban life as we know it today. Instead of thinking of how to repair the design of an existing urban center, we do better to begin from scratch: what should be the principles of design of an urban-industrial center? In the greater part, the choice of this benchmark brings into consideration the implications of the kinds of technologies which will characterize the environment in which cities thirty to fifty and more years ahead will exist. These are the technologies which make possible powered interplanetary flight. These are the technologies which enable us to construct simulated Earth-like environments on the Moon and Mars. These are the technologies which will provide the power, the tools, and the biological production for life and work in such simulated Earth-like environments. Reflecting on what the design of and life within such cities must be, forces our attention to view similarly urban-industrial life on Earth under the conditions implicit in the same technologies.

Technologies may be revolutionized, but the basic principle of the family household cannot be changed without destroying society. Therefore, technology changes will be obliged to adapt to the axiomatics of internal functions of the household, and the social functions of the households and their individual members within the community and society at large. Hence, if a new city is planned, and its construction begun today, and if that city's planning is properly referenced to the impact of the cited technologies, that city will be functional, if maintained properly, one, two, and more hundreds of years ahead. People live in household units, and they move from place to place in the course of the day, as well as requiring the movement of delivery of goods and services into the household unit or reasonable proximity. The physical space minimally required for household units is defined, and so forth and so on. Relative to households whose cultural level corresponds to a 25-year-old school-leaving age today, the parameters of the optimal household unit's spatial allotments have not changed essentially in the history of civilization, and will not during the coming several hundred years. As noted, taking into account the impact of cited technologies over the interval thirty to fifty years ahead, we have implicitly all of the parameters city planners and architects should require to design a city to live for a thousand years.

On Earth, as on the Moon or Mars, instead of laying

structures upon plots of land, in the fashion practiced still today, the city's construction should be begun with construction of a common foundation: a single honeycomb of perhaps three tiers, within which subsurface movement of people, freight, and services will flow, into the indefinite future. This must be very durable, to last for many centuries, and must be modular, capable of adapting to changes in technology of movement without alteration of the foundation in which those movements are located. The educational and related cultural functions should occupy the center of the city built upon the foundation, flanked by the central governmental and related functions. The area of the city proper should probably be circular (at least, in the functional sense of physical space-time of movements), with the industries located outside the rim of the city. Cities should be of finite sizes; population expansion should be accommodated in additional such cities, cities functionally interdependent linked by transportation trunkways of high-speed (magnetic levitation?) rapid transit. The city should be a total environment for living and associated householder's functions, durable to persist without changes in this aspect of its function for many centuries.

The initial cost per household unit for such a city might appear costly at first. Think of this cost per household as capital-intensity, and think also of the major part maintenance represents in the costs of operating a city. The object is economy of labor, through a durable city maintained at ever-lower social cost.

By increasing the operatives' component of the labor force to approximately 50%, and forcing realization of the benefits of economy of labor in a "science-driver" mode, such cities are feasible propositions for the period immediately ahead, and much superior to attempts to repair existing cities which are inherently costly to maintain and poorly designed as to function. If a city, such as decayed New York City, were to be rebuilt, the recommended approach is to checkerboard the city as it exists, building in each checkerboard the kind of foundation-up development indicated, according to a general plan respecting the ultimate result. Think always of the fact that doubling the percentile of the labor force employed as operatives, under conditions of rapidly advancing technology (economy of labor) means more than doubling the average productivity of the total labor force, and means that we can afford twice as much and more, per member of the labor force as a whole. *Think not of what we are doing, but of what we ought to be doing,* including the cited $3 trillion repair bill for infrastructure which we must spend during the immediate years ahead, in any case, if we are not to die collapsing on a pile of rubble.

Water is life. Fresh water is indispensable for life of plants, animals, and mankind on land. The ratios per kilogram of biomass grown are well-established parameters. The distribution, and redistribution, of existing surface and ground supplies and throughputs of fresh water, delivers the water to the place it is optimally required. This distribution increases the relative potential for a square kilometer of area. We must not only distribute water supplies; we must manufacture them. Controlled thermonuclear fusion will render this production of fresh-water supplies economical . . . and so forth and so on. Production and distribution of energy supplies is of the same general significance; this increases the relative potential for a square kilometer of area. Transportation and communications have the same effect, *in proportion to the level of physical goods output per capita.* The development of *urban-industrial infrastructure has the highest relative potential.* Thus, improvement and maintenance of infrastructure makes possible the increase of the potential relative population-density. That is the general functional significance of that capital-goods subcategory called basic economic infrastructure. Hence the close correlation between rates of improvement of infrastructure and rises in productivity.

NOTES

1. The writer specified the preconditions for a computer-based
economic forecasting system during a December, 1978 seminar
in New York City. The central requirement specified for this
application of the writer's forecasting method was the model
of Riemann's cited 1859 treatise. Because of the importance of
that treatise and its outgrowths for plasma physics and related
matters, the development of the computer-based forecasting
method was undertaken as a joint project of the weekly news-
magazine *Executive Intelligence Review* and the Fusion Energy
Foundation. The writer supplied the specifications for the model,
including the system of linear inequalities to be used for Na-
tional-Income Accounting preparation of data, and the hydrothermodynamic functions' specifications. The economics-
finance section of the *Executive Intelligence Review* prepared
the data base. A team headed by FEF's Director of Research,
Uwe Parpart-Henke, directed the development of the mathematical applications for the computer application. A combined
team of the two entities conducted the programming and the
computer runs themselves. As the historicial data base has been
developed back into the nineteenth century, and the forecasting
has been extended to the data bases of foreign nations, special
computer-assisted studies were added, and results obtained
through these special studies added as features to the basic
forecasting methods and procedures. The indicated result was
a 1981–1982 series of studies of energy-flux density parameters, historically, for various aspects of the economic process.

2. The 1863 date references such developments in Britain as Prince
Albert's intervention, but also, more importantly, the impact
of the Russian Czar Alexander II's unveiling his military alliance
with President Lincoln. Russian naval fleets were dispatched
to New York and San Francisco harbors, and a stiff note sent
to Lords Palmerston and Russell in London, warning that Russia would make war in Europe if Britain and Napoleon III
launched their projected military intervention on the side of
the Confederacy. (Britain, France, and Spain had conquered

Mexico, and had imposed the puppet-emperor Maximilian Hapsburg to supervise the killing and looting of the Mexican people.) Britain abandoned its military adventures against the United States and Mexico, and, apart from threat of an alliance against the United States by Britain and Japan during the immediate aftermath of World War I, Britain dropped the policy of military subjugation of the United States which it had maintained since 1763.

The documentation, based on primary sources, for most of the following review of the liberal Establishment "families," is found in A. Chaitkin, *Treason In America*.

3. Sir John Robison is best known in the United States for his book, *The Roots of Conspiracy*, 1796–1797. This book, a hoax, has been reprinted by the John Birch Society, itself a modern echo of the treasonous "Essex Junto" of the early nineteenth century in ideology and ultimate sponsorship. Robison, a British SIS agent, formerly associated with SIS's Russian service, was operating out of Edinburgh at the time of the book's writing and publication in the United States. The book had the following significance at that time. Lord Shelburne's East India Company circles were collaborating closely with the Swiss and Jesuit circles behind the Jacobin movement in France; hence, the Swiss British agent, Albert Gallatin, later a member of Jefferson's and Madison's cabinet, was organizing Jacobin insurrections in Pennsylvania, for example. In an effort to cover up the British role in steering the Jacobin operations inside the United States, and to drive a wedge between the United States and its friends in France, Robison wrote the lying book, purporting to prove that it was implicitly the allies of Carnot and Lafayette who were responsible for the interventions. Even Washington was deceived. Later, John Quincy Adams and others uncovered the fraud of Robison's book, reporting to President Jefferson (in then-U.S. Senator Adams' case) that it was Robison's friends who were the center of the treasonous enterprises.

4. As Chaitkin documents, Caleb Cushing of Newburyport (Massachusetts), the interface between the leaders of the Massa-

chusetts-based Abolitionist movement and the Charleston Confederate conspiracy, negotiated with his Confederacy plotters the rigged election of Franklin Pierce; the Buchanan election was rigged through the same channels.

5. Judah Benjamin was, together with August Belmont of New York City, a key British agent within the Confederacy. Later, resuming British citizenship, from London Benjamin organized the founding of the Ku Klux Klan (1867) and its initial funding. Benjamin's political career has a single characteristic: the attempt to destroy the United States from within. For an insight into his mental processes, see his 1868 "Treatise on the Law of Sale of Personal Property."

6. The Lincoln assassination was a joint British Secret Intelligence Service-Jesuit (e.g., Surratt family) plot. Circumstantial evidence points suspicion of complicity at Secretary of War Stanton, who stripped the President's personal security to one officer, called away from the door to the President's box at the relevant moment. Midstream in the trials following the assassination, the investigation was suppressed. Relevant documentation remains sealed to the present date.

7. The key issue behind the Lincoln assassination is most efficiently identified by the content of the President's last public address, of April 11, 1865, three days before his assassination: "We all agree that the seceded States, so called, are out of their proper relation with the Union; and that the sole object of the government, civil and military, in regard to these States is to again get them into that proper practical relation. I believe it is not only possible, but in fact, easier, to do this, without deciding, or even considering, whether these states have ever been out of the Union, than with it. Finding themselves safely at home, it would be utterly immaterial whether they had ever been abroad. Let us all join in doing the acts necessary to restoring the proper practical relations between these states and the Union; and each forever after, innocently indulge his own opinion whether, in doing the acts, he brought the States from without, into the Union, or only gave them proper assistance, they never having been out of it." (*Collected Works,* Vol. VIII, New Brunswick, 1953, p. 403.)

With Lincoln only beginning his second term, as long as he remained alive, the Carpetbaggers' looting of the occupied states would not have been possible.

8. *Cf.* Salisbury, *op. cit, passim,* on the circumstances of the Specie Resumption Act.

9. On Theodore Roosevelt's pro-British and pro-Confederacy outlook, see Chaitkin, *op. cit.*

10. The Colonel House-E. H. Harriman connection is relevant to the case of Wilson. By running as a third-party candidate, Theodore Roosevelt threw the election to Wilson, thus ensuring the passage of the Federal Reserve Act, and U.S. commitment to join Britain in a World War against Germany.

11. Documentation on the Harrimans' fascist and racist backgrounds, and Senator Moynihan as a backer of Harrimanite racialism, was published by the New York U.S. senatorial campaign of Melvin Klenetsky, during 1982. *Cf.* Chaitkin, *op. cit.*

12. There are exceptions to this general rule. The case of Carroll Quigley's *The Tragedy and The Hope* is illustrative of a writer with a sense, at least, of how matters actually proceed. There are also some candid, detailed admissions, such as Marilyn Ferguson's *The Aquarian Conspiracy;* on this, *cf.* Carol White, *The New Dark Ages Conspiracy.*

CHAPTER 10
Briefly, On Inflation

At first glance, there are two kinds of inflation: *cost-inflation* and *monetary inflation*. The first is inflation seen as a rise of costs from inside the process of production of physical goods; the second is seen as a rise of prices irrespective of changes in the paid-out costs incurred by their production.

If we assume the case for the hypothetical, consolidated agro-industrial enterprise, that the social ratios of employment of the labor force's components do not change, but that prices of physical goods rise, this would typify monetary inflation. If the increase in prices does not exceed the rise in unit costs determined by a shift of composition within the labor force, this would typify cost-inflation.

In fact, such "pure types," occurring independently of one another, do not occur in the real world. In the real world, tendencies whose nature is that of monetary inflation cause cost-inflation, and those tendencies whose nature is that of cost-inflation cause monetary inflation, or depressions' deflation.

The crux of the matter is a point on which we have already touched, earlier in the text. We locate that point in the present light.

Money put into circulation, or money substitutes (such as paper negotiable for money, credit taken as payment—and as claim against money), goes somewhere, and is ultimately presented as a claim for tangible wealth or labor. For example, payment of money taken on account of financial usury, or ground-rent, is part of the Waste component of Overhead Expense. It goes into the hands of the recipient, *in return for nothing*. There is no "exchange"; there is merely a taking.

The obligation to pay such claims, by production and distribution of physical goods, by paid labor, and so forth, is a
tax added implicitly to the price of everything. Costs rise
accordingly; cost pressures push up prices. The economy is
paying more for its total output, and receiving nothing in
return. *Inflation.* Yet, someone receives this money, and pre-
sents it as a claim for payment in tangible wealth or labor,
somewhere.

　　True, it is likely that it will be recirculated as the basis
for more usury, more ground-rent payment, and so forth.
Like a cancer, usury grows to relatively larger proportions in
the economy, and sucks out increasing percentiles of the money
income of the economy. This depresses purchases for physical
goods and services: stagnation combined with inflation tends
to be the result on which this sort of cancer converges, if
unchecked. A few years back, some wags coined the term
"stagflation" for this sort of development. Still, the fund of
money stocks in the hands of the usurers increases, taking
from the economy's total money flows at an increasing rate.
Inflation increases.

　　A bubble in ground-rent, perhaps, is organized by the
usurers. Rents rise, reflecting increasing ground-rent components. A real-estate market shaped by price-earnings ratios,
skyrockets the price of the land upon which buildings stand.
Industry moves out, unable to bear such augmented ground-
rent costs. Middle-income households move out, leaving the
very poor behind and some of the urban wealthy and rich.
The cost of wages zooms in the area affected, reflecting the
costs of zooming ground-rents added to rent. The industries
move away more rapidly, and their employees, too. Only high-
gain industries employing the very poor remain as a remnant
of industry.

　　Money of usury buys out more and more of the economy's ownership, while the households employed in usury
and the enterprises of usury, consume increasing amounts of
physical goods and Economic portions of Overhead Expense.

So, the structure of the economy's social and productive processes are changed. The compositions of components of National Income accounts change. Now, the inflation takes the form of a cost-inflation.

Some fellow spreads the rumor, that "too rapid a rate of growth causes inflation." He may produce charts and graphs to document his argument. It is all utter nonsense. Naturally, if the cancer of usury (and other Waste elements of Overhead Expense) has reached the stage that its share of the growth of the money supply is growing relative to the rest of the economy, monetary expansion will feed Waste more rapidly than other aspects of the economy. Thus, efforts to stimulate real growth correlate, under those conditions, with increase of the rate of inflation.

Imagine a gang of murderers is lurking along a road between one town and the other, ambushing and killing many of the travelers along that route. Under such conditions, what would one say of the expert who reported to have statistical proof that the increase in the death rate of the two towns was caused by travel between the two?

The methods for dealing with inflation are:

1) Promote a high rate of technological progress in production of increased physical-goods output.
2) Allow the increase of money supply to flow to nothing but loans for appropriate categories of investment, as we indicated earlier.
3) Tax the income of usury and related Waste items of Overhead Expense into extinction.

About the Author

Lyndon H. LaRouche, Jr. was born in 1922 in Rochester, New Hampshire. After completing military service in the China-Burma theater, he left university studies to begin a management-consulting career in 1947.

In 1974, LaRouche founded an international news agency which published the political newsweekly *Executive Intelligence Review*. Since October 1979, *EIR* has issued regular quarterly forecasts which have proven themselves the only competent ones among all government and private econometric services.

His proposals for monetary reform and his strategic policies have made the subject perhaps the most controversial international public figure currently, and certainly the most controversial figure outside the ranks of present and former officials of governments.

Since October 1979, LaRouche has publicly advocated the development of defensive energy-beam weapons, since only with the help of this technology, which can annihilate enemy missiles in flight, can the doctrine of "Mutually Assured Destruction" be superseded. In February 1982, LaRouche spoke on this subject at an *EIR* seminar in Washington, D.C., attended by leading Americans and Soviets. In March 1983, President Ronald Reagan announced that the development and deployment of space-based defensive beam weapons was now the official policy of the United States.

LaRouche is advisory chairman emeritus of the National Democratic Policy Committee (NDPC), the fastest-growing political action committee within the U.S. Democratic Party. The NDPC is backing 2,500 candidates at the local, state, and national level, as of May 1984.

In 1980, LaRouche ran for the Democratic presidential nomination on the platform of a program for overcoming the economic crisis, in the tradition of the "American System" of Alexander Hamilton. LaRouche's campaign organization for the 1984 Democratic presidential nomination, The LaRouche Campaign, is organizing a broad movement behind him. The focal points of LaRouche's policy are his support for the development of defensive energy-beam weapons and his battle for a new world economic order on the basis of the most modern technology, centered on giant agro-industrial projects. The editors of the *EIR* published a biography of LaRouche in July 1983 under the title *Will This Man Become President?*